hed is our t
mil
mc

D1037990

CIVIL-MILITARY RELATIONSHIPS
IN AMERICAN LIFE

CIVIL-MILITARY RELATIONSHIPS in AMERICAN LIFE

JEROME G. KERWIN *Editor*

THE UNIVERSITY OF CHICAGO PRESS
CHICAGO · ILLINOIS

CHARLES R. WALGREEN FOUNDATION LECTURES

THE UNIVERSITY OF CHICAGO PRESS, CHICAGO 37
Cambridge University Press, London, N.W. 1, England
W. J. Gage & Co., Limited, Toronto 2B, Canada

FOREWORD

✻

LECTURES given at the University of Chicago under the Charles R. Walgreen Foundation for the Study of American Institutions are designed to assist students toward an understanding of contemporary life in the United States—its background in history; its ideals, values, and institutions; its present needs and possible future. To foster an intelligent citizenship and patriotism, not narrowly nationalistic in their expression and with thought and knowledge much more than emotion as their basis, is a principal purpose of this Foundation.

During the year 1946–47 the Walgreen Foundation has presented four series of lectures; the present volume constitutes one of these series. As groups of addresses, they were prepared for delivery to audiences of students. As separate volumes they, in similar manner, particularly invite laymen and not specialists to be their readers. In their published form they represent an effort of the Walgreen Foundation to extend its usefulness beyond the limits of the University of Chicago campus.

Without the gracious co-operation of the authors and of the University of Chicago Press, this effort could not have been made. Mrs. Carol Taylor aided greatly in preparing the manuscripts for publication.

JEROME G. KERWIN

Executive Secretary, Charles R. Walgreen Foundation
for the Study of American Institutions

INTRODUCTION

✳

NO TRADITION in American institutions is better established than the supremacy of civilian control of our government in war as well as in peace.

The founding fathers insisted that the commander-in-chief of our armed forces be the president of the United States, a civilian elected by the people. From the very beginning of the Constitution, George Washington, in spite of his many years as general of the Revolutionary Armies, scrupulously observed the spirit and letter of their mandate. After his election as president, he rarely appeared in military uniform and at all times recognized in word and action the supremacy of civil power. Abraham Lincoln, during the greatest crisis in the history of our country, vigorously asserted the predominancy of civil authority over military officers, to whom great power had been delegated, and maintained this position even when they entered the political field and became his active rivals. His famous letter to General Hooker evidences his acute awareness of the threat to democratic institutions implicit in the seizure of civil power by military officers. We cannot be confident that the matter can be left to the conscience of individual military leaders in spite of conspicuous examples of appreciation of our basic freedoms from Washington to Lee and from Jackson to Eisenhower.

One does not have to look far afield for examples of military usurpation in democracies. Such may be found in ancient and modern history in all parts of the world. In our own Southern Hemisphere the history of the American republics contains an endless repetition of coups d'état led by military figures.

The United States has been free—perhaps too free—of military consciousness in peacetime. Most wars have found us hopelessly unprepared and with a scorn for military men and military problems which made us slow to give them the necessary material, manpower, and authority. It was part of a young and remote republic's best tradition for over a century to decry the standing armies of Europe with their conscript or mercenary forces and to deplore the aristocratic privileges, the overbearing demeanor, and, above all, the influence on national policy of a professional officer caste. Like Mirabeau we felt that "Prussia is not a state possessing an army but an army possessing a state." By the end of the nineteenth century we had begun to acquire a considerable naval establishment, but our army before the Spanish-American War was weak and devoted largely to occupying garrisons in remote areas and reminiscing about the Indian wars. After each war we have quickly discarded many of our military resources.

The postwar policy of the United States is without precedent. It is a policy of maintaining large-scale military preparation until such time as the foundations of international organizations dedicated to preserving the peace of the world are a firm and dependable substitute for national force. The dreadful new technology has convinced us that time, space, and oceans are no more dependable bulwarks of national security than a Maginot Line. We still appear to have a monopoly of the ultimate weapon; but scientists tell us that this is only for a very brief period, and our very monopoly gives us an insight into its powers for instant attack and total destruction. Accordingly, we enter the postwar period with the greatest army and navy in our history, a total military force of over a million men and larger appropriations for army, navy, air forces, and scientific research for military purposes than for the entire pre-war federal budget.

This new situation in American history presents a new problem to the American people. How shall we maintain civilian control of our foreign and domestic decisions in the face of a world situation which requires vast military establishments and equipment and inevitably large delegation of authority to and great control of new weapons and resources in the hands of a professional military group?

We have already taken the first step by placing the authority over the manufacture and production of atomic weapons, as well as atomic energy for civilian purposes, in the hands of a civilian board. However, many great powers of an unprecedented nature continue in military control. Many of these influences are subtle. Much scientific research is still under military jurisdiction. Universities, colleges, and other research institutions are more and more becoming dependent on military sources for research grants. Informed and patriotic scientists have expressed profound doubt as to the progress of fundamental research that can be made under military supervision. The postwar military establishment approaches in size and complexity the ones we have heretofore maintained only in wartime. Although for the present we are relying on voluntary enlistments, the possibility of eventual adoption of compulsory service for training in peacetime is by no means foreclosed. The size of the officer cadre required for these large establishments not only will be an influence in itself but will inevitably place greater emphasis on military science and training in the colleges and universities of the country. An unprecedented number of veterans in our civilian community, and particularly their organized spokesmen, produce a military consciousness in spite of temporary reactions against military life upon their return to civilian occupations. A sizable proportion of American industry is receiving army, navy, and air-force contracts, and industry has a larger stake in military orders than in any previous peacetime era. And, finally, the recent loose federation of the War and Navy departments with the separate new department for air, unless very carefully administered, may have the unexpected and unfortunate results of both weakening our preparedness and increasing the influence of professional military men in matters of public policy.

The purpose of the essays in this volume resulting from a series of lectures made possible by the Walgreen Foundation is twofold. It is to identify the change in conditions which has caused a much greater pervasiveness of the military in American life and at the same time to raise the question of how our cherished freedoms can be preserved by the safeguarding of the predominancy of civilian power. Although some aspects of this question have been treated in fragmentary fashion by specialists in various fields and were dramatized in one field during the debates on atomic legislation, this is the first attempt to identify the many facets as part of a single problem in American political institutions. Although the volume is a valuable contribution, it is but a preface to the subject. Its main value should be to stimulate others to study, write, and publish on this important but neglected topic. The dilemma of avoiding militarism and of maintaining our democratic institutions while at the same time keeping well prepared presents the American people with one of the major political problems in the history of the United States.

HERBERT EMMERICH

PUBLIC ADMINISTRATION CLEARING HOUSE
March 1, 1948

TABLE OF CONTENTS

SCIENCE, TECHNOLOGY, AND WAR

WALDEMAR KAEMPFFERT

*

EVER since the emergence of *Homo sapiens*, there never has been a time when there was not some science and some technology. Peking man, half ape though he was, knew the use of fire, which implies that he was enough of an experimental scientist to discover that heat can boil water and bake meat. The primitive who first made a spear by thrusting one end of a stick into a fire and who fashioned knives and other implements out of bone and flint was a technologist. It must have been a highly gifted inventor who first raised a sail on a dugout canoe or who devised the fire drill. There were Edisons enough a hundred thousand years ago, for they invented weaving, pottery, brewing, and a hundred other arts.

If it took experimental science and technology thousands of years to progress, it was because of taboos, superstitions, and reliance on magic. Experimentation teaches nothing without objectivity, and complete objectivity was impossible without a change in outlook, a change in culture. Even Hellenistic science was not free from primitive animism, and it was so saturated with philosophy and a contempt for material things that mathematics, especially geometry, was more cultivated than experimentation. The practical Romans, great engineers, were so dominated by Greek philosophy that their contributions to physics and chemistry were not outstanding. Experimenting is often dirty work; and when work was dirty, Greeks and Romans left it to slaves and craftsmen. Not until

1

the rumblings of democracy were heard was it possible for experimental science to rise.

Liberalism as we know it was born in the Renaissance. It is no accident, then, that in the fifteenth century objective experimenting in the modern sense began. The culture was changing, and so was the outlook. Inquiring minds turned from heaven to earth, from salvation to the improvement of man's lot in life. The voyages of Columbus and of the circumnavigators who came after him testify to a romantic spirit of adventure, nursed by the trader's interest in profits.

Books enough have been written on the relation of trade to the rise of science. Trade is essentially democratic. It makes no distinction between Asiatics and Europeans, Englishmen or Italians. At the trader's counter or the bank-teller's window lord and commoner are equal. There is no doubt that trade and science developed hand in hand. But trade is always accompanied by war, and it was never possible to separate the exigencies of war from those of trade. Modern science would have evolved without war, but the record indicates that the impetus to scientific experimentation came from war.

According to Sorokin, there have been 902 wars and 1,615 internal disturbances in twenty-five hundred years. After the fifteenth century warfare tends to become more scientific and mechanical, armies grow in size, the military demand on industry increases, until in our own time the civilian, industrial population and the fighting forces constitute almost a unit. Moreover, wars increase in frequency as science and technology advance. The most bellicose period in all history is the first half of the twentieth century. A burgher of the Middle Ages had sixty-five hundred more chances of dying peacefully in bed than has his European descendant of 1946.

The East has had its wars as well as the West. Yet the East was always more pacific than the West. Despite its clashes with the outer barbarians, despite bloody dynastic upheavals,

China for several thousand years regarded the soldier as a ruffian and relegated him to a low rung on the social ladder. In Europe the soldier was glorified, even ennobled. It is significant that ethics comes out of the East and techniques come out of the West.

The art of waging war remained static in the West after the fall of the Roman Empire until the introduction of gunpowder. As strategists, as tacticians, as inventors of fighting equipment, the Romans had achieved the utmost. If warfare was to be improved, it needed more power—power that did not come from human or animal muscles. Gunpowder furnished that power. Thereafter war assumed a new aspect and experimental science was stimulated.

Volumes have been written on the cultural influence of the steam engine on the assumption that for the first time it gave the technologist a source of energy that was not "free" in the sense that the wind, falling water, or animal power is "free." But gunpowder is potential energy of that kind—chemical energy. Its invention antedates that of the steam engine by about four centuries. The officers who first battered down strongholds and slew their enemies by the hundreds with artillery and muskets instead of by the dozen with spears, arrows, and swords did not realize that they were dealing with chemical energy.

Gunpowder came to Europe out of China either late in the thirteenth century or early in the fourteenth. At first, bombs and grenades were used. It took generations before artillery appeared and more generations before it was efficient. The first practical artillery pieces were of bronze, an alloy of copper and tin, two scarce and expensive metals.

It was inevitable that ultimately iron, abundant in almost every country, would displace bronze. Exactly when and where the substitution was made is not known. The place was probably western Germany, eastern France, or Belgium; the time about 1410. It is probably more than a coincidence that artillery was developed during the Renaissance, a period when the European mind was thinking and speculating as it had not done since the halcyon days of Greece. Historians of the Renaissance dwell on the bold thinking of Galileo and other physicists of the period and on experiments with crude steam engines—the exploration of physics. There is a connection between this interest in experimental science and gunpowder.

The early iron-founders were not industrialists but artisans. Their small furnaces were fired by charcoal and blown by bellows worked by water wheels. Such was the rising consumption of charcoal and such the Continental demand for long, English cast-iron artillery, considered the best, that, in the reign of Henry VIII, who began preparations for war immediately on ascending the throne, England's forests were threatened. By the middle of the seventeenth century it was economically imperative to substitute coal for charcoal as a foundry fuel.

The substitution of coal for charcoal was no easy matter. Raw coal cannot be used to smelt iron. Neither can raw wood. Undesirable organic compounds are driven from wood by what the chemist calls "destructive distillation." Thus the iron-founder obtained the more or less pure carbon that he needed for the smelting of ore. To make coke from coal by the same process was no great step. More striking was the invention of the blast furnace. The combination of blast furnace and coke oven changed the whole character of iron-founding. By the end of the seventeenth century iron was cast on something like a quantity basis, and England led the world in cannon-making. Industrialism was on the march. So were banking and financial capitalism, with all the two imply so far as credit and corporate enterprises are concerned. In the fabric of our technological culture, science, industry, and financial capitalism are inextricably interwoven.

Modern European warfare and business are based on coal and iron, and both became military necessities after the invention of gunpowder and the introduction of cannon and muskets. This influence of military needs on metallurgy persists. Bessemer made it plain in his autobiography that the inefficiency of cannon in the Crimean War and the need of steel prompted him to invent his converter. The first tough, strong steel alloys were developed for the protection of battleships, with the result that the first sound automobiles were those with shafts and gears of nickel steel. Indeed, most of the great advances in metallurgy were made under military pressure. The best crucible steels, for example, were long produced in quantity by Krupp, and Krupp for many years led the world in the production of electric-furnace steel. With the advent of the military airplane and airship the need for aluminum alloys was urgent, so that a new branch of metallurgy was opened. Much the same story can be told of magnesium and beryllium.

The coal needed for coke ovens of early iron-founders was mined in open pits, which were soon flooded by springs. A way had to be found to drain the mines. Horse pumps were first used. They had their serious limitations, and horses were expensive. Out of the need came the Newcomen-Savery pump, and out of the Newcomen-Savery pump came Watt's condensing steam engine. Link by link the chain of inventions that joins gunpowder with iron cannon, iron cannon with coal, coal with steam pumps and steam engines, is forged. Once American Indians froze to death on a ledge of outcropping coal. After the steam engine, nations could not wage war effectively without coal. The last link in the chain that joins science to war is the fission of uranium, followed by the destruction of two Japanese cities, the tests of Bikini, the plans of engineers to substitute "piles" of uranium for coal and oil in driving the machinery of powerhouses. That the rapid achievement of uranium fission was the direct result of the last war it is unnecessary to emphasize.

Would all these innovations in metallurgy and engineering have come to pass without benefit of war? Probably. But the process would certainly have been slower. It is noteworthy that as soon as Hahn and Strassman had split the uranium atom late in 1938, the great powers thought first of the military importance of what had been done. It is also noteworthy that, after radium was discovered and its spontaneous release of energy observed, physicists were already thinking in terms of an atomic war. In 1938 no physicists was willing to declare that atomic energy would be a military or an industrial reality in less than half a century. Yet in a few years, and by the mobilization of all first-rate university physicists and by the expenditure of two billions, uranium had become a military problem and a problem in international politics. No nation would have spent two billions on physics in a few years merely for the academic pleasure of converting part of the uranium atom into energy.

If the thesis that Western science came out of war, specifically out of the invention of gunpowder, needs any additional proof, we find it in the history of industry, particularly in the improvement of the musket. We think that specialization in industry, the partition of labor, is a characteristic of the industrial revolution. But by the sixteenth century muskets were produced on something like a factory basis. Even women made some of the parts, just as they made munitions in recent world wars. By 1540 Hartmann of Nuremberg had standardized calibers (the relation of length to bore); by the end of the sixteenth century the musket-makers of Augsburg could offer to the Duke of Milan nine hundred "hand tubes" all designed to fire balls of the same size; and by 1775 all firearms fired standard bullets. About this time artillery wheels were standardized. All this is important because standardization is the very essence of mass production. And standardization grew out of military necessity four centuries ago. It follows that powder and musket works were about the first to assume a modern industrial aspect and that governments undertook the production of explosives, munitions, and military equipment. Oak Ridge and Hanford, where we are making atomic bombs, had their small-scale counterparts all over Europe before the Declaration of Independence was signed.

Specialization and standardization were soon introduced in warfare. A fieldpiece or a musket is no weapon for an untrained soldier. Cannon must be grouped in batteries and musketeers in companies; and if they are so grouped, the supply of ammunition must be systematic. What we call "artillery preparation" demands a plan of procedure. There must be supervision by competent officers. Some science is demanded in laying fieldpieces. Since the manipulation of artillery could not be left to raw conscripts and to officers who knew nothing of ballistics, organization was clearly demanded. The standing army of today became a necessity when gunpowder was introduced. Cannons and muskets are machines; and whether machines are found in the factory or on the battlefield, they can be used effectively only by a permanent force of trained men. Drilling and standardization of weapons breed solidarity. Uniform a standing army and the solidarity is heightened. It follows that armies, organized, trained, and uniformed as they were after gunpowder made its appearance, were very different from the motley contingents of serfs that feudal barons conscripted in response to the summons of an overlord. In feudal times there were no batallions, regiments, and brigades, very little drilling, and nothing like a closely knit force that fought as a unit. Battles were scarcely more than encounters between armed mobs, with little control after the fighting began. Even a siege was conducted with far less organization and efficiency than a conflagration is extinguished by a modern company of municipal firemen.

It was not the desirability of distinguishing friend from foe that led military leaders to adopt uniforms but the necessity of converting an armed force into a living machine. Frederick the Great insisted on this point. Even in his time remnants of feudal laxity persisted. He could voice nothing but contempt for the Great Elector's troops because of their slipshod appearance, their poor equipment, their lack of order. "No uniform, no discipline," was his comment.

When even small principalities and duchies framed specifications for cloth which had to be one quality and color, the hit-and-miss system of craft production broke down. An order for ten thousand uniforms or pairs of shoes was huge. For an army of one hundred thousand, more than six hundred thousand ells of cloth were required, and the entire annual output of the West Riding, center of England's cloth industry in the eighteenth century, was only twenty-five thousand. During the Seven Years' War weavers were unable to meet the demand for military cloth. So it was with the production of wagons, boots, harnesses, hats, and belts. Russia proceeded to fill some of her needs in state factories. In most Western countries the army dealt with contractors whose duty it was to control the quality and color of cloth. In the early nineteenth century we hear of the sewing machine. It was Thimonnier's, and it was first used in making army uniforms (1829).

This demand for uniforms had its ancillary effects. There was an enormous military demand for dyes, soap, detergents, and bleaching agents. When prices soared in 1775, the French Academy of Science offered a prize of 2,400 livres for a process whereby soda could be made cheaply. Nicolas Leblanc, a pupil of Lavoisier, won it and thus started the heavy-chemical industry on its course. His discovery was as important for industrial chemistry as Watt's invention for mechanical engineering. It follows from this that the clothing industry of today, which makes suits, hats, and shoes by the million, is a direct offspring of the eighteenth century's demand for uniforms.

Mass production demands not only standardization but the interchangeability of machine elements and parts of products. We take it for granted that in thousands of shops we can buy an electric lamp that can be screwed into a standardized socket or a standardized nut that will fit a standardized, threaded bolt. Interchangeability is a great invention. Like standardization it is the child of military necessity.

The first step in this direction was taken by the English to supply pulley blocks for the Navy. A single full-rigged ship needed about fifteen hundred, and the Admiralty was purchasing about one hundred thousand annually after the middle of the eighteenth century. Samuel Bentham saw to it that woodworking machines performed specific functions in a series of operations, with the result that pulley blocks were standardized and made interchangeable. The principle was independently conceived and applied for other purposes by Leblanc in France (1785). Much impressed, Jefferson did his unsuccessful best "to get the U.S. to bring him over," which he was ready to do on moderate terms. It remained for Eli Whitney to reinvent and reintroduce on a larger and more dramatic scale the most important of all manufacturing principles. He is the technological ancestor of the industrialists who produce bathtubs, automobiles, electric lamps, vacuum cleaners, bottles, and containers in trainload lots. He was not thinking in terms of peace. In 1798 he received a government contract to make ten thousand muskets. Before the eyes of an astonished group in the War Department, he assembled a dozen muskets from a heterogeneous mass of parts. But the machine tools that made the parts had also to be invented, and this Whitney did. The machine tools of today are variants of those that he designed for his military purpose. With him begins that wholesale transference of skill to the machine which distinguishes quantity production.

Even before Whitney's feat Watt had been perplexed by the problem of boring cylinders for his first steam engines. But one man in all England could meet his requirements, and he was a cannon-borer, crusty John Wilkinson. Had it not been for Wilkinson's improvement of common-boring machinery, the steam engine would not have appeared when it did. It became in turn necessary to standardize screw threads and all machine-tool operations. To the military use of gunpowder we must therefore attribute that rise in the specialization of tools which marks the organization of manufacturing.

This trend toward the standardization of military and industrial equipment had its influence on transportation. Industries had grown around coal and iron mines which had been opened up to meet the demand, largely military, for metal. It was natural to connect mills with markets. When the locomotive was at last developed to a state of practical perfection, the military began to think of railways in terms of the transportation of troops. In a small country like Great Britain it was enough to connect town with town. On the Continent tacticians thought of frontiers and rapid movement. This thinking gained strength after our Civil War, during which troops were moved for the first time on rails. The roads of the Roman Empire were military roads. The railroads of western Europe were superimposed on these ancient Roman roads for the most part.

The tales that have come down of the huge armies assembled by Xerxes, Darius, and Attila are myths. Until railways were laid, the largest force ever assembled was the Grande Armée of five hundred thousand men with which Napoleon invaded Russia and which he had conscripted in almost every country west of Russia. It marched not in a solid mass but in separate corps. Because there were no railways, it could not be adequately fed and clothed, for which reason it floundered in the mud and starved and froze to death during the retreat from Moscow. Even in the war of 1870 Von Moltke required nine railways to deploy a force of four hundred thousand men and to control a reserve of one hundred thousand—a feat that would have been impossible without the telegraph. If an army of a million men could be assembled and shifted about without railroads and other engine-driven vehicles and without telegraphs and telephones, the slaughter would probably be no worse than it was with bows and arrows, spears and pikes.

This influence of gunpowder and cannon on land has its counterpart in naval history. Did English foreign trade increase almost 300 per cent between 1613 and 1700 because the Navy had grown in power? Or did the Navy increase in power because foreign trade was expanding? On the whole, it is likely that the mounting of cannon on ships provided the stronger stimulus. If larger warships can be built to mount more cannon, then larger merchant ships are bound to keep pace. Nor must it be overlooked that the merchantmen of the East India and other companies of the time were armed.

Our fast transatlantic steamers certainly testify to the influence of war on shipbuilding. It is not the fast liner that makes the most money but the slower cargo carrier. It was through subsidies that the "Queen Mary," "Queen Elizabeth," and the "Normandie" were built, and all three were designed not only as passenger carriers but as troop carriers.

Nor should it be forgotten that aviation was developed in its early stages with military support. It was the French general staff that gave Ader, French inventor of an unsuccessful flying machine, his chance. Langley was able to build his man-carrying machines with the aid of a congressional appropriation made at the behest of the military. It was the Army again that displayed more interest in the Wright brothers' invention than any industrial company. The zeppelin was the invention of a Prussian officer who thought primarily of war and only incidentally of competing with steamships and railway trains.

This same influence of military necessity is apparent in civil engineering. In every country, ours included, the military exercise a strict control over navigable rivers and regulate the heights of bridges. Napoleon was captivated by the idea of digging a tunnel under the English Channel, probably because he thought it would simplify the invasion of England. Because they also thought in terms of war, the English have steadfastly opposed the construction of a tunnel, even though it could be easily blocked or flooded. Had that tunnel been built, the British Army could have escaped more easily than it did after retreat from Dunkerque. Though the commercial benefits that would accrue to the world by digging canals through the isthmuses of Suez and Panama were stressed by promoters, military and naval advantages were the main considerations.

It may be argued that we have merely enumerated a series of empirical discoveries and inventions which have been applied in waging war, that soldiers have always taken what they needed. What, then, of theoretical science? There is no obvious relation between the kinetic theory of gases and the slaughter of fifty thousand men in battle, between the laws of gravitation and the defeat of the German fleet off Jutland in the first World War, between the exploration of the earth's atmosphere and military necessity. Yet the relation is there, concealed but tangible.

Even a university scientist cannot insulate his mind against the needs and tensions of society. There is not a branch of physics and chemistry that has not felt the influence of war.

Theorists do not grope for problems to solve; the problems are presented by society. When the steam engine was invented, physicists naturally studied it, measured the amount of coal required to generate a horse-power per hour, theorized on the conversion of potential energy into kinetic energy, and finally arrived at the conclusion that heat is a form of energy. Thus was thermodynamics born. Out of thermodynamics came clear indications of more economical methods of utilizing coal and hence more efficient steam engines, which was exactly what industry wanted. The factory owners were provided with better engines merely because engines presented interesting scientific problems and because costs could be kept within reason if coal were saved.

It was to be expected that the interest of the theoretical scientist would be similarly aroused by gunpowder and cannon. Robert K. Merton and others have dwelt on this aid that even the most pacific scientists lend to the soldier. Concern with the expansion of the gas generated by gunpowder, the combustibility of powder, the strength of metals used to make cannon, accounts for the solution of what Merton calls "derivative problems." Often the experimenters know nothing of the original military impetus and imagine that they are conducting research purely for the sake of adding to the sum total of human knowledge.

Scientists and engineers of the fifteenth century were more aware of their relation to the soldier than are our theoretical physicists. Leibnitz, Denis Papin, Otto von Guericke, and a score of other seventeenth-century scientific and philosophic celebrities all dabbled in what they frankly called "military mechanics." Galileo was a professor of military science whose formulation of the laws of falling bodies was the logical consequence of a successful solution of the problems presented by the trajectories of artillery projectiles. B. Hessen, a Russian physicist, has shown that the laws of gravitation came as much out of ballistics and out of better means of determining longitude as they did out of experiments with swinging pendulums or the motion of the moon. Only in the French artillery schools was science taught systematically in the eighteenth century, and it was in one of these that Napoleon received his education.

We have no space to explore the relation of biology to war. It is enough to point out that epidemiology grew out of the military necessity of dealing with typhus and similar infectious diseases and that needs of the second World War impelled the military to mobilize bacteriologists and chemists whose task it was to discover antimalarials which would take the place of quinine, to introduce an influenza vaccine, to study tropical diseases intensively, to introduce DDT, to make the most of plasma and its protein constituents.

If the biological sciences have lagged behind the physical sciences, the reason is plain. Military advantage and profits lie in the physical sciences but not in the biological sciences; and the connection between war and profits has been set forth by economists time and time again. The biological sciences of agriculture and medicine are not exceptions to the rule; the connection of both with war and profits is obvious.

An army is a highly organized and planned artificial society. Like the civilian society of peace, it is subject to tradition, and it resists technological change. The phenomenon of "cultural lag" appeared—Professor William F. Ogburn's term for the time that invariably elapses between the discovery of a new principle or machine and its acceptance and practical application. Since war is a matter of life and death, victory or defeat, it might be supposed that new death-dealing inventions would be eagerly sought. But innate opposition to change is an inherent in soldiers as it is in financiers and industrialists.

Generations passed before the musket completely displaced the bow and arrow, the spear, and the pike. The Chevalier Bayard, *sans peur et sans reproche*, hacked off the right hands of captive musketeers but treated captive archers, swordsmen, and pikemen with knightly courtesy. Despite all the efforts of Bessemer to substitute steel for cast iron in casting cannon, Woolwich arsenal rebuffed him; and it was not until 1882 that British artillery was made of steel. Though the merits of the Burnside breechloader had been tested along with about twenty others and had demonstrated its efficiency as early as 1857, the Civil War was fought with muzzle-loaders. What were the reasons for opposition? Among them were inaccuracy of fire, rapid heating of the barrel, the impossibility of cleaning the bore after every shot, waste of ammunition because of the rapidity of fire. And all this despite the success of the Colt revolver. It was not until 1865, when the Civil War was almost over, that seventy thousand breech-loading Spenders were ordered.

The machine gun has a similar history. Maxim had to hawk his model all over Europe and succeeded in selling it only after it was taken up by Zaharoff, a high-pressure salesman of munitions who later became the chairman of Vickers-Maxim. Similarly, every important European power rejected the built-up gun. Though Krupp was the leader in military and industrial metallurgy, he found it difficult before 1904 to sell his wares to armies at home and abroad. Ironclad ships had been tested by our government as early as 1846, and the French used them successfully against Russian forts at Kinburn in the Crimean War. Nevertheless, Ericsson had to build the "Monitor" at his own expense to defeat the "Merrimac," an old hulk hastily covered with railroad iron. Even the revolving turret of the "Monitor" was not new.

Despite the successful use of the captive balloon for reconnaissance during the Civil War, general staffs could see little in the first successful airplane. The Wright machine was at first rejected by this country, Great Britain, and France. It might be supposed that after the airplane had been used for bombing during World War I, opposition to its further use would die.

Yet in 1919 the United States Army issued a pamphlet in which it was concluded that "contrary to general belief outside military circles the principal function of the airplane is the securing of information with fatal accuracy." At the trial held in Riom in 1942 to discover who was to blame for the collapse of France during the second World War, testimony was offered to show that none other than Maréchal Pétain, despite his experience, had systematically opposed the formation of a large air force. Gas might have been used in battle at any time after the French Revolution, but it remained for Fritz Haber, an industrial chemist, to suggest that chlorine be wafted at Ypres and Neuve Chapelle. It was only later that mustard gas, known for sixty years, was fired from shells.

There was less cultural lag in science during the war recently ended than in any of its predecessors. The reason is to be found in the way research was organized. In the past the military dominated research. Even before war was declared on the Axis powers, President Roosevelt had created the National Defense Research Committee, later merged into the Office of Scientific Research and Development. Civilian scientists sat with representatives of the Army and Navy on various boards, but the civilians outnumbered the military. Hence the boldness of thinking and of experimentation. As a result, World War II ended with more innovations than did World War I. No new principles were evolved—not even in the atomic bomb—because there was no time for fundamental research. But years were telescoped into months, months into weeks, because accumulated knowledge was exploited systematically as never before.

We have only to look about us to note what has happened. Electronic devices control industrial processes with a new precision. Television has been brought to a new pitch of perfection. Radar has made it possible to detect hostile bombers from afar and to fight naval battles in the blackest night, to reflect signals from the moon, to prevent collisions at sea, to make aviation safer. Synthetic rubber has been produced from alcohol and petroleum gases. Plastics have been developed as substitutes for metal and wood. Jet and rocket propulsion have increased the speed of airplanes. The tropical diseases have been subjected to better control. Penicillin has been extracted from molds on an industrial scale, and a whole series of new antibiotics has been discovered. DDT powder has stripped typhus of its old terror and controls insect pests with ease. And the crowning achievement has been the release of energy from uranium.

The lesson taught by organized research to reach a military goal has made a deep impression. What will happen if we are plunged into another war two or three decades hence? There will be no time to organize our scientific and industrial resources if atomic bombs are hurled at us across the ocean or carried on planes that have a range of ten thousand miles; no time to raise, equip, and drill a huge army. Peace, too, imposes scientific and technical obligations. To meet these, nationally supported research is as necessary as it is in time of war. An effort to pass a bill which would have given us a National Science Foundation failed in the last Congress. That effort is bound to be renewed. Indeed it was the fear of another global war that inspired Senator Harley Kilgore to introduce the bill that failed to pass.

The scientists supported the National Science Foundation bill because it was so framed that they would not be conscripted in peace. But some of them balked at the inclusion of the social sciences in the research program. And the reason? Research in the social sciences spells trouble—political trouble. Yet the social and the natural scientists worked admirably together during the war in conducting what is called "operational research." Economists, geographers, and weather experts co-operated with technicians familiar with airplanes and bombing in mapping the targets for strategic bombing. Similar co-operation was found necessary when it was discovered that general staffs were unable to use most effectively the weapons and explosives with which they had been supplied. Social scientists were called in to find out what was wrong. They discovered that what had been supplied was not always what commanders at the front thought that they wanted. As a result of team work between the social scientists and the technical experts, the army concluded that it would be best to supply not weapons which approximated an ideal but weapons that could be effectively used with other equipment on hand.

Governments and industrial organizations would probably learn through operational research, in which social scientists participated, not only what is the best type of material or machine to achieve an end but whether the end itself is worth achieving. Combine the natural and social sciences rationally, and we even lay the foundation for a science of civilization.

The social sciences cannot be much longer neglected as we neglected them when, through organized research, we devised the atomic bomb. Horrified at their own success, the atomic physicists have plunged into international politics and hence into the social sciences. Even at this late day the Atomic Energy Commission of the United Nations does not lean so heavily as it should on the social scientists. The inquiries of that body have been conducted largely by physicists, the heads of industrial corporations, and well-meaning, public-spirited citizens who know nothing of the forces that shape history. And the larger issue of abolishing war itself has hardly been touched—an issue that cannot be left to the military or to the diplomats who serve national interests or to manufacturing corporations. It is an issue that must be studied by the social scientists with the aid of economists, psychologists, professional soldiers, natural scientists, and technologists. It is surely a paradox that we enlisted the aid of psychologists and social scientists in making the most of operational research during the war but still decline to use them in settling the most momentous issue that mankind must face.

FROM SOLDIER TO CITIZEN

DIXON WECTER

✣

VETERANS of the second World War comprise ninety-three million people. Sixty-three million served under flags of the United Nations, and of these nearly sixteen million were Americans. These latter were represented on the stage of the San Francisco Opera House in April, 1945, when seventeen young men and women from the Armed Forces stood at attention when the first session of the United Nations opened. In the deliberations that followed they played no part, but their presence seemed a healthier, more self-confident symbol than that of the little band of wounded veterans of the first World War who with tardy sentiment were invited to witness the signing of a *fait accompli*, the Versailles Treaty. As still another innovation, among the more than fifty consultative committees which moved as satellites of the Assembly, representatives of veterans' organizations raised at least a minor voice, while the ranks of the American delegation included a young former governor who had served with distinction in the Pacific. The main decisions made possible by youth's victory, for the determination of youth's future, still rested as always with the noncombatant and the over-age.

"Youth for action, old age for wisdom," is a hoary proverb, but its ring seems a little less assertive than formerly. A generation which faced its disillusionment before the shooting began—which had sometimes taken the Oxford pledge of pacifism and had often refused to don the glittering mail of the crusader, however efficiently it might adopt battle dress and jungle camouflage—appeared, at least in segments, to be of

19

more skeptical temper and with more sober responsibility than any articulate groups remembered from earlier wars. For example, a veterans' organization met last summer in Des Moines; at its close the chief of police remarked that this was the first convention in the city's history where "not a single delegate wound up on the police blotter." And there were G.I.'s of the rank and file spotlighted by fame who certainly seemed more liberal, dissenting, or rebellious than most foot-sloggers of past wars—like Bill Mauldin, the Army's favorite cartoonist, whose pen was now devoted to the mordant ironies of Willie and Joe's readjustment to civil life; or Sergeant George Baker, creator of the Sad Sack, who took an active part in the earnest program of the American Veterans Committee; or Marion Hargrove, who organized a Legion post that the Legion did not want and who, when invited to address the National Association of Manufacturers, delivered himself of a speech called "See Here, Private Enterprise."

To claim that such behavior is typical of the sixteen million, or a majority of them, would be rash. The mass of veterans, like the mass of American citizens, probably respond to economic issues only when they impinge upon the individual pocketbook nerve and tend on the whole to regard politics as rather less exciting than baseball. It may be regrettable, but even the impact of a global war in which they fought well and bravely seems not greatly to have shaken this basic attitude. But let us take refuge, in the beginning, in the reminder of that French maxim, "All generalizations are false, including this one." In the files of the War and Navy departments are masses of data about the men who composed the Armed Forces of our greatest war—facts anthropometric, medical, psychological, educational, vocational, which one may contemplate until dizzy with the possibilities of writing monographs about the typical American and perhaps to prove any thesis he pleases. Has it not been remarked that some sociologists rely upon statistics as a drunk leans against a lamppost—more for support than for illumination?

"The typical American veteran" is a myth. He springs from the most heterogeneous people of the Western world; he is all sorts and conditions of men. These sixteen million vibrate in sections, like a long bridge, and this is as it should be, both as a demonstration of democracy and for the nation's equilibrium and safety. Upon certain matters veterans are a little different from their elders: such, for example, as better schooling—two-thirds having gone beyond grade school, as compared with one fifth of Pershing's A.E.F.—and their youth, spent largely in the shadow of the Great Depression and under the New Deal, which may help to explain why three out of five servicemen (in states keeping separate tabulation) voted for Roosevelt in 1944 and why they set more store upon economic security than earlier generations of American veterans and rarely appear to be afraid of what their elders call "state paternalism." These factors, of course, are mainly independent of war service and may conceivably outweigh its influence.

In respect to this service, there was every diversity imaginable—from arctic to tropics, five continents and seven seas, cargo boats that lolloped across the Pacific in five weeks and fighter planes in which experience was accumulated at the rate of four hundred miles an hour. There is no stereotype here. Two out of three Americans in the Armed Forces went abroad, but only half were ever stationed in combat zones; only one out of eight actively opposes an enemy on the firing-line.

To the great majority, however, war was a huge educational experience, for learning at an accelerated pace about new technologies, foreign languages, geography, the races of mankind, and often about the tensile strength of human nature, one's own and one's fellows', often under fatigue and fear, within the frame of a vast system whose organization was as

complicated as its objective was simple. Toward this one overwhelming purpose, defeat of the enemy, all the soldier's days
and nights, his thoughts and conditioned reflexes, were
channeled; and its withdrawal is one of the obvious reasons
for the veteran's common complaint that civil life at first
seems bewildering, aimless, centrifugal. This feeling is a very
old one. For instance, one of Pershing's veterans wrote, late in
1919, for a paper called the *Home Sector:* "We are dissatisfied
with the mere earning of our daily bread, bored with the
conditions we once yearned for, moving on, amid swirls of
dust of our own raising, on toward—what? A great leader
could tell us. . . . Will the year 1920 see such a leader emerge
from the crowd?" To this particular question, time held an
ironic answer: Warren G. Harding. Not long ago an earnest,
intelligent group of young veterans went to Washington to
offer themselves to the service of the federal government—
feeling what the Quakers would call "a concern" for the postwar world, as strong as that which had led them to volunteer
five years before—but they found that beyond a few jobs of
clerical routine in the State Department there was literally
nothing for them to do.

The veteran's return to civil life is always an anticlimax, if
not a disenchantment, the road back from hero to house-
holder. He has idealized and been idealized during absence.
He returns to a housing shortage, now affecting an estimated
four million veterans, where vagabondage, discomfort, and
"doubling up" always make for bitterness. And, after the
complete economic security of Army life, he faces the wave of
inflation which (as they said in 1919) seems to have only one
advantage: a man without a dollar is fifty cents better off than
he used to be. At my university in California some homeless
G.I.'s are reported to have been sleeping in all-night movies
and parked cars, yet their grade-point average ranges from a
tenth to a full point higher than the pre-war undergraduate

average, which by and large would seem to exempt them from the category which your Chancellor Hutchins has termed "educational hobos." The next season's crop of veterans will be younger and perhaps less serious minded, but so far the work done in our colleges and universities above and beyond the requirements of the Veterans Administration has been a pleasant surprise to many educators.

On the other hand, no one should be surprised at the bumper harvest of divorces already begun, which will certainly continue through the next few years—as happened before in the wake of war marriages in 1918 and the postwar unions of 1919. During the war an Army pamphlet about war brides ventured (with humor all too rare in the War Department) to quote the old definition of a wife as "a person who sticks by you in trouble you wouldn't have had if you hadn't married her." It now appears that this definition is imprecise, and a toll of desertions and broken homes will be paid for the haste, emotional strains, and derangements of five years' mobilization.

In postwar relationships there is also a touch of the old irritation toward stay-at-homes, "the rat-race of civil life," as veterans call it, and traditional murmurs about profiteering and lush wages, which just as inevitably will serve as the fulcrum for a national bonus. But the rift between veterans and organized labor—foretold with anxiety in some circles, glee in others—has failed to materialize. The psychiatric rate among veterans is also rising, although the Veterans Administration seems wary about disclosure of statistics. Of course, it can be exaggerated—among other reasons, because several million Americans who had not heard of neuropsychiatry in 1940 now know about it. In regard to that old apprehension, the veteran and the crime rate, the facts do not warrant alarm: teaching a soldier to shoot Germans or Japanese under the rules of war does not mean that he will come home and shoot his old neighbor on sight. In the vacuum left by dearth of war news, daily newspapers always tend to play up domestic crime; and, of course, the very label "veteran" enhances human interest and melodrama at group expense. Even so, results are by no means sensational.

Not activity but inaction is the chief complaint of civilian faultfinders at the present time. Taking advantage of unemployment compensation under the G.I. Bill of Rights, approximately two million veterans were lately receiving such benefits, some for a few weeks and others for several months. This is more than twice the number enrolled under the educational provisions of the bill. "Resting up awhile" may be a very normal thing to do, but the presence in our midst of the self-styled "52–20 club" leaves a sour taste with the taxpayer, an unfair prejudice when chalked up against the majority. It recalls a word three hundred years old for loafing on the job—"soldiering."

The most striking fact to report concerning veterans' readjustment, however, is the almost universal eagerness of the serviceman to submerge his identity in civilian habits. Segregation, conspicuousness, hallmarks of the military caste, are definitely not wanted. The saturation point, reached by the close of the war, has now become surfeit. Clothing salesmen report that Army veterans avoid purchase of brown suits and Navy veterans of blue. Protective coloration is what the average ex-serviceman now wants in attitudes as well. This nation stands in no danger from masses of soldiers who refuse psychologically to demobilize—the seed plot from which sprang the totalitarian revolutions of a generation ago. Our recurrent complaint is not the maintenance of tension but a fatal facility for relaxing, our penchant for "normalcy," which someone has described as the expectation that things should be again as they never quite were.

The soldier, too, is the victim of this national nostalgia—

although as a child of the depression, the C.C.C. and N.Y.A., and of war's incertitude, he is probably a good deal less sure than his father that rugged individualism and economic nationalism are the keys to this paradise. He tends to look toward the government to do things for him which he cannot easily do for himself, acquiescing in a theory which regards government as a positive instrument for welfare rather than as one whose business is a negative or police function. And this, whether the young veteran votes Republican or Democratic; for, whether he recognizes it or not, this aspect of the New Deal has become a lasting part of the American scene. A Republican is now a man who promises the more abundant life at bargain rates. Whether he can deliver, the next two years may help to prove. The success story, whose brightness has hypnotized generations of American youth, is for the veteran a little tarnished, the gospel of self-help a little less cogent. Such, at least, was the report by welfare workers, educators, public-opinion polls in the latter thirties and early forties; and it seems likely that military service—a world of competence rather than of competition, where needs are met and decisions made from the top—has not reversed this drift.

Although foxholes, air warfare, commando raids, operation of radar, and other complicated techniques left a larger area to self-reliance than did the trench warfare of 1917, yet in the field of ideas, argument, persuasion, compromise, the Army remains much as it has always been—an efficient mechanism for action, not thought. The military mind sees the world in black and white: a gun is either perfectly clean or else dirty enough to merit a tongue-lashing, a man is either fit to fight or fit for the hospital. Under this conditioning the soldier learns to live by fact rather than by reasoning, to obey, not to question why. "Keep 'em ignorant," was the classic officers' precept in the first World War.

In this war, thanks to the pioneering work of General Ben

Lear, an orientation program was launched, with special officers, talks, discussion groups, and movies like the "Why We Fight Series," which appealed to the growing visual-mindedness of Americans. It addressed some of the broader problems that made similar groups in the British Army such exciting schools of citizenship—the background of the modern world, the foreground of individual responsibility. The blueprints and top leadership of this program were admirable, but on the whole it was an admitted failure. So says Colonel Benjamin Bowker, chief of orientation, in his recent book called *Out of Uniform*. It started too late, had to build upon too shaky a base of previous education for the discussion of ideas, and as it spread through the ramifications of Army and Navy had to rely for effectiveness upon commanding officers—the older professionals tending to derision—and upon personnel too often clumsy, cowed, and incompetent. In unskilled hands the program turned into propaganda, a word and concept against which the child of the thirties reacted with convulsive allergy, since he took it to mean that somebody was trying to put something over on him. A young marine who lost an eye in the landings on Guam, now a scholarship student at Harvard and a leader in the American Veterans Committee, told me (in a judgment confirmed elsewhere) that the sincere convictions of the G.I. as to why he fought were usually drawn from influences outside the service—his own thinking and reading, bull sessions with friends—rather than through "channels."

A few sentimentalists have supposed that the returning soldiers bring with them the knowledge, breadth, and wisdom necessary to settle the problems of this nation and to consolidate the victory. In sober truth it must be said that veterans no more than civilians know all the answers, the incantations to bring forth a just and lasting peace. The closest they come to unanimity is their satisfaction in getting back to the United

States and civil life. Having seen the world, they are convinced that home is best. "When you come down to it," writes a youthful veteran, "anybody born in the United States starts so far ahead of all the others that it's a wonder any of them ever catch up!" In so far as this sentiment is a tribute to the sanitary superiority of the United States, it is innocent enough; so far as it means the freedoms and opportunities of a democracy, it is fine; but so far as it becomes mere nationalistic brag, it is something less lovely. Some veterans will tell you in a moment what the Limeys are like, because they spent a few weeks in London; others admit to similar clairvoyance about the Frogs, and so on around the world. Too often a single incident, as being cheated by a shopkeeper, can color the verdict passed upon a whole race.

The converse impression left by the veteran himself rarely occurs to him. Yet with his generous, easygoing ways, his high degree of literacy, his aptitude for machines, his passion for children, his fondness for ice cream and movies and comic-books, his sentimental idealism, and his cynicism, and also let it be said his not uncommon bumptiousness and unsubtlety about matters like drink and women, he stands in the eyes of Europe and Asia as a microcosm of America.

One curious trait of the young American is observed by a soldier who spent forty months in the Southwest Pacific. "The G.I.," he writes, "has never learned to express himself in words. Language to him expresses emotions, not ideas." Hence he is prone to speak in one way, to act in another. Often he talks negatively, profanely, even brutally—as if he were prejudiced or stupid—but he acts with tolerance, thoughtfulness, and understanding. To the uninitiate, this is a hard nut to crack. Regrettable incidents have occurred and will occur, so long as armies of occupation remain, but it is assuring to know that the effect of long exposure is often salutary. One questionnaire showed that after three months in

Britain thirty-seven soldiers out of a hundred disliked or were irritated by the British, but after a year's residence only 7 per cent of the same group disliked the British, although fifteen still admitted irritation. On the whole, our foreign policy will probably benefit.

In respect to the domestic scene, one of the most bewildering contrasts upon the soldier's return is that between the conformity of the military world, in dress, reactions, patterns of obedience—with only a faint obbligato of what the G.I. called "bitching"—and the uproarious forensic hubbub of civil life. A Navy man on leave in the autumn of 1944 wrote:

I came back to find the air and the public prints seething with epithets, accusations, charges, and contentions involving the government—labor, industry, religions, races. . . . I had . . . been away so long it assumed distorted proportions in my mind. It seemed to me that the country was divided. Everybody seemed to hate everybody else. I wanted to know why in the hell these Statesiders couldn't get along as we did out there. I had forgotten what presidential elections were like . . . that election had to pound me over the head to make me realize that this is still a free country, and that most Americans like to prove it by disagreeing with the powers that be.

Temporarily unaccustomed to the democratic processes, the young veteran may react in one of two ways. He may ask: "Oh, what's the use? It's all political pull, and run by a machine. My vote and influence don't matter a damn." Hence a rather widespread lethargy or indifference toward politics. This recoil often takes the shape of skepticism or cynicism—one veteran remarking that elections find the soldier "looking under the band of the campaign cigar." On the other hand, conditioned to action and group solidarity, the veteran and his friends sometimes take law and justice into their own hands. They have not yet learned that short cuts frequently turn into blind alleys. Captain Shays and his embattled farmers in 1786, the Bonus Army in 1932, found this out at some cost of lives. At Athens, Tennessee, last August an angry band of G.I.'s at gun's point forced a fair count of the ballots on election day and thus turned out of office a corrupt machine of ten years' standing. As usual, the vigilante spirit got out of hand, with shootings and car-wreckings by armed bands. The resort to violence was obviously wrong, but since the law itself proved dilatory in letting a minority rule illegally and since appeals to the governor had been fruitless, at least the ends came fairly close to justifying the means. With this lesson still fresh, officials at Malvern, Arkansas, took steps to forestall a similar coup by veterans against a machine eighteen years old: a court order was swiftly issued giving veterans' representatives the legal right to witness the vote-counting, while state police stood on guard. The result was another victory for the new ticket against the machine. At the worst, this is good citizenship gone berserk.

In most situations the veteran has little need to throw his weight around. Contrary to proverb, republics are not ungrateful, and from the beginning of this nation veterans and their groups have been powerful instruments in the field of force called public opinion—witness the history of national leadership from Washington, Old Hickory, and Zachary Taylor to the succession of seven soldier-presidents (broken only by Cleveland and dimmed in battle record solely by the non-combatant Chester A. Arthur) who stretch between Andrew Johnson and William Howard Taft. Modern times have displayed less devotion to the man on horseback—partly because the conditions of war have unseated him, while the managerial revolution has altered his role to something less dashing. The veterans of World War I who have been nominated for, or occupied, the presidency, namely, Lieutenant Landon, Captain Willkie, and Major Truman, owed little or nothing to military glamour. It might be remarked that veterans are likely to be less impressed by the mere fact of a war record

than are civilians. Early in 1920 a poll among twelve thousand
ex-doughboys on the question of a military man for president
reported three thousand affirmative votes, nine thousand negative. While a minority thought that "a soldier would straight-
en things out," on the other side a frequent comment ran, "I
have had enough of military domineering."

On the other hand, the civilian tends to vote for almost any
soldier whose candidacy is well managed—whether from
patriotism, gratitude, hero-worship, or a covert sense of guilt.
The close of this last war saw twenty-two veterans of it already sitting in Congress. A great many more were on the way;
within ten to fifteen years their leadership would be decisive.
On the eve of the recent election, the Republican National
Committee announced that, whereas their opponents had put
up only sixty-three veterans as congressional candidates, they
themselves were offering a hundred and ten, including three
veterans of all three last wars, beginning with Cuba in 1898, a
record of service and a debt to be paid that seemed well-nigh
overwhelming. There might come a time, as happened in some
midwestern states under the glut of Civil War veterans, when
a man might choose to conceal his war record because he was
ashamed of the political exploitation which such things
endured. Of these World War II veterans running for Congress,
only sixty-nine were elected; frequently, of course, veterans
were pitted against each other. But, counting veterans of
World Wars I and II, the new Congress will number about
forty-nine in the Senate, two hundred in the House.

In past times the veteran's public role has always been inseparable from the organizations which he forms with those
who "have drunk from the same canteen." Internally these
clubs have rarely been schools for democracy or disinterested
citizenship. I do not speak of the now-antiquated idea of a
club "for officers only" with hereditary notions, like the
Cincinnati, Military Order of the Loyal Legion, or Naval and

Military Order of the Spanish-American War, which luckily are likely to turn into nothing more sinister then genealogical societies. But the great veterans' organizations, the Grand Army of the Republic, Veterans of Foreign Wars, and the American Legion, have always been directed by "professional veterans" at the top. Important decisions are reached in committees and caucuses; a façade of sometimes deceptive unanimity is presented to the public. Much of the fault, of course, lies with the average convention-goer, more interested in seeing old friends and in high jinks than in matters of politics and policy. Entrenchment and seniority count for a great deal. In the Legion today the heavily outnumbered veterans of World War I still remain firmly in the driver's seat and probably will continue so until they are sure that their three million neophytes can be trusted to drive contentedly within the same ruts.

Such organizations, in fact, tend to prefer the safe to the experimental. This attitude may come in part from the veteran's reaction against the anxieties and crises of his youth and in part from the assumption of leadership by prosperous dues-paying, reunion-attending members. Organized veterans are prone to regard themselves as sentinels of the nation permanently on duty—a fine feeling in itself, but sometimes the collective pugnacity that follows military training plus the behavior of groups makes their patriotism a chip on the shoulder. The G.A.R. waved the Bloody Shirt in many a political campaign, advising its boys in blue to "vote as you shot," while their late adversaries, the United Confederate Veterans, licked their wounds and dwelt lovingly upon the Lost Cause. The Legion made itself the special champion of "one hundred per cent Americanism"; in the early twenties National Commander Alvin Owsley brashly told a newspaper reporter: "Do not forget that the Fascisti are to Italy what the American Legion is to the United States." With considerable justice,

however, veterans' organizations have always resented that
pacifism which comes to debunk our wars—portraying us
either as dupes or bullies and helping to confuse the national
morale and foreign policy.

The "gimme complex" is identified in many minds with the
organized veteran. President Benjamin Harrison's needless in-
junction to his G.A.R. Commissioner of Pensions to "be
liberal with the boys" and in reply the enthusiastic pledge to
"drive a six-mule team through the Treasury" belong to a day
when the rising pension outlay was geared to the high protective tariff, so that a multitude of ex-soldiers farming in the
West who should have been low-tariff men continued faith-
fully to stand by the Republican platform. The Legion is, of
course, identified with bonus policies which it contrived to
carry over the vetoes of four such diverse presidents as Harding, Coolidge, Hoover, and Roosevelt. Thanks also to Legion-
sponsored legislation, our pensioners of the first World War
increased 866 per cent between 1919 and 1929, at a time when
the number of European pensioners from that war was steadily
diminishing. In the United States alone has war service per se
been established as a compensable claim and have hospitalization benefits been wholly divorced from service-incurred in-
juries or impoverished old age.

In such matters it is nobler to err on the side of generosity
rather than of parsimony, but one thinks at times that the
pressure of veterans' organizations for bigger and better benefits has not always truly represented the veteran's best interests, his role as a taxpayer in his own right, or the cause of
civilian good will. Memories of the bonus fight and its share
in what is commonly called "the veterans' racket" are still
prejudicial to the Legion's reputation. Seven states—Illinois,
Michigan, New York, Rhode Island, Massachusetts, Ver-
mont, and New Hampshire—have lately approved bonuses,
with only Maine rejecting, while New Jersey, Texas, and

California indorsed housing, loan, and land-settlement schemes. Another national bonus is not far away. In 1906 Mark Twain wrote an unfinished fragment called "The Fall of the Great Republic," in which he foretold a revolution led by "the Prodigy," a shoemaker who beguiled the masses and built a dictatorship upon the veteran vote, "for every pensioner had a vote, and every man and woman who had ever been acquainted with a soldier was a pensioner; pensioners were dated back to the Fall, and hordes of men who had never handled a weapon in their lives came forward and drew three hundred years' back pay."

We all recognize the justice of replanting the veteran in civil life, of promptly compensating him for real losses and putting him abreast of the stay-at-homes both by education and by certain economic aids, and of giving every practicable assistance to the war-disabled. The veteran now has special benefits of retraining, life and unemployment insurance, civil service preference, reasonable guaranty of his old job, federally insured loans, hospitalization, domiciliary care, and burial allowance—which in effect means that (besides five million veterans of previous wars) sixteen million citizens are now living under a domestic Beveridge plan which in any other context would be viewed with alarm as the entering wedge for state socialism. Most of these things are just and in the best traditions of American generosity. But to set up highly invidious distinctions, such as the superseniority advocated by certain veterans' groups but wisely rejected last June by the Supreme Court, is to breed bitterness and to do veteran-civilian relations a lasting disservice.

Certain politicians, of course, will always be found trying to thumb a ride on the veterans' bandwagon. All pressure groups, including the Communist party of America, are currently seeking to exploit the veteran, his rights, his claim upon public good will, his hopes, and his discontents for all they are worth, apart from his own best interests and those of the nation. The C.P.A., which began by instructing the faithful to bore into the Legion, now advises them to join everything else in sight. Lincoln once told a group of Wisconsin farmers that he could not imagine why politicians were always flattering the farmers—unless it was because the farmers cast so many votes. Today he might say the same of the veteran. To haul a veterans' group into every debatable issue, local or national, is the quickest way of destroying its power for those rare occasions when it needs to pull its weight. Any veterans' group should beware of any professedly friendly boarding-party that tries to capture it.

Sometimes the bait offered is too gross for all save the most gullible. Thus, Father Coughlin has his St. Sebastian's Brigade for veterans; and on the other side of the fence are the Protestant War Veterans headed by Edward J. Smythe, sedition-trial defendant and anti-Semite; Joe McWilliams offers his Servicemen's Reconstruction Plan proposing a $7,800 bonus; Gerald L. K. Smith has his Nationalist Veterans of World War II as an adjunct to America First. Fieldman for the last-named organization is one George Vose, a veteran to be sure, who was court-martialed for selling week-end passes to fellow-soldiers and for retailing United States government property. Former Senator Robert Rice Reynolds also makes a big play for servicemen in his American Nationalist party. Talmadge's Georgia, home of the Ku Klux Klan which first addressed young Confederate veterans and later the veterans of World War I, has lately spawned "the benevolent and patriotic society" of Columbians, a band of khaki shirts whose organizer is Homer Loomis, young veteran from New York City who announces that at home "I learned to hate Jews and Negroes." Their cult is "Americanism," the kind which means putting the fear of God into other people. Groups of this kind sometimes appeal to the young demobilized soldier, craving a little more excitement and the lure of regalia and mass action. Not infrequently the transient in uniform, like the northern serviceman in the South, the country boy in the big city, the American soldier in Germany, tends to pick up the prejudices of his new environment rather than to lose his old ones. As is often said, one rotten apple can infect a dozen sound ones, whereas a dozen good ones have never been known to make one rotten apple sound. We Americans like to think of ourselves as men and women of good will. But each of us bears within himself the dormant virus of mob cruelty, race prejudice, and hatred. Only a healthy state of mind, among civilians and servicemen alike, can keep these germs from multiplying.

In fine contrast to the attitude just mentioned was the stand taken three years ago by the Disabled American Veterans, upholding the rights to full citizenship of American soldiers of Japanese ancestry and the pressure—from veteran and civic opinion—which caused the names of Japanese-American servicemen to be restored to the Roll of Honor, after their removal by local prejudice, in a Pacific Northwest town. The newly organized American Veterans Committee in its Des Moines convention last summer went on record demanding fair play and proper compensation for the Nisei forcibly removed from their western homes during the war years, in recent months successfully broke the Navy ban against enlistment of the Nisei, and protested the new War Department order suspending enlistment of Negroes in the Army. The poll tax and mob violence have also been subjects of its pronouncements.

The A.V.C., which has grown during the past year from twelve to nearly eighty thousand members, is the most heartening development among veterans of World War II. Its running mate, the Amvets, which is about the same size, has done useful work among local chapters—particularly in the

Middle West, where it is strongest—but its national program seems vague and stodgy. The A.V.C., which happens to be liveliest in the cities, has spoken clearly and firmly upon a number of issues: strongly favoring the United Nations as a step to world government with teeth in it, fair-employment practices, scrupulous respect for civil liberties, and enforcement of its motto, "Citizens first, veterans afterward." It seems that in each postwar period there is a healthy recoil against the abuses of previous veterans' organizations: first, the politically nonpartisan Legion against the G.A.R. and now, the A.V.C. against the veteran-partisanship of the Legion. It remains a minority group but, after all, no veterans' organization has ever attracted more than a minority of the servicemen who fought in any war of our history.

So far the A.V.C. has numbered its recruits by the tens of thousands to the Legion's new millions; probably this ratio will remain. The men most in sympathy with a liberal group like the A.V.C. are temperamentally the nonjoiners, as has been remarked by its chairman, Charles Bolté—a convert from isolationism who left Dartmouth to join the British Army before Pearl Harbor, lost a leg at El Alamein, and returned to throw his intelligence and enthusiasm into this group. His organization played a large part in overturning the long-somnolent regime of General Frank T. Hines in the Veterans Administration, and the succession of General Omar Bradley, "the G.I.'s general," who in the face of official Legion opposition has done so much to implement the federal veterans' program.

The A.V.C. is now engaged in an internal and apparently winning struggle against the Communists in its ranks—not in the old emotional spirit of Red-baiting but under a firm, intelligent determination to escape the dominion of a group which takes orders from sources outside the United States. In their stress upon full employment, checks and balances between labor and management, extension of social security, and the outlawing of racial discrimination, the leaders of the A.V.C. appear to recognize that the health of the union is the best insurance against the spread of domestic communism. Thomas L. Stokes, well-known newspaperman, who covered the first convention of this organization last summer, described it as "a fine antidote for the cynicism beginning to spread again through America and the world."

The maintenance of several veterans' groups to attract servicemen as diverse in their interests as glad-handers of the Legion and the V.F.W., middle-of-the-roaders of the Amvets, the thoughtful liberals of the A.V.C., together with special units, like the Disabled American Veterans, Military Order of the Purple Heart, and the various divisional outfits, seems on the whole a salutary thing. The political potency of collective veterans is very great; but as has also been suggested, their interests and inclinations are by no means uniform. Furthermore, through a wise economy of nature, in a democracy when the prize of power becomes too great and too attractive, competition for leadership begins, and fragmentation is the result. Some are bound to be pressure groups, espousing aims which other citizens may think unwise or irrelevant to the cause of organized veterans—but pressure groups, seemingly inseparable from democratic government, may be either good or evil, and in the multiplicity of their pressures there is considerable safety.

The older veterans' organizations need this competition, just as they have sometimes needed in past days to recollect the cardinal principle of citizenship—namely, that the welfare of the veteran is enmeshed with the good of the whole United States. What benefits the country will benefit him and vice versa. We have come to see that jobs enough, production and consumption, civil liberties at home, and responsibility in the new world order are everybody's business. The decade of the thirties witnessed a domestic debacle that sprang largely from blind selfishness to the bond between group welfare and the satisfactions of the individual; it closed with the beginning of a global war bred by the equally stubborn refusal of many nations to admit the tie between their security and the good estate of all. The commonweal of peoples and the commonalty of man are the two concepts which emerge most clearly, which must unite rather than segregate both nations and groups within those nations.

Will the veteran and his civilian neighbor ever begin to question the rightfulness, the necessity, of the war lately ended, as happened in the wake of the previous World War? Whether rightly or wrongly, the leaders of both—Woodrow Wilson and his protégé Franklin Roosevelt—chose to present the war aims in a medium of crystalline idealism: a world to be made safe for democracy, and for those components of democracy the Four Freedoms. This interpretation fitted their own temperaments and their presuppositions about the romantic feeling of most Americans on the subject of war. So, comparatively little was said about self-defense, about simple self-interest. This interpretation runs two risks: first, that some soldiers may not comprehend or may readily forget the necessity for their war and its intimate relationship to the life and safety of the nation; second, that the dissolution of high purpose and group unity, which always follows victory, will engulf the meaning and validity of this achievement. Wars of self-defense speak for themselves, but, because America's part in two great wars has been largely extra-territorial, we often begin to decide, after the danger is past, that there was no danger.

But the chief peril of dwelling for awhile upon this high moral plateau is that we begin excessively to idealize both ourselves and our co-workers. In this interdependent world we save ourselves by saving others, preserve our own democracy by fighting its threat afar off. Then, with the war over, perhaps by way of compensating for the discovery that we ourselves are not so perfect, we begin to find our allies something less than we claimed for them—and wreck the mythologies of which we rather than they were the makers. Britain, we see, is still carrying the white man's burden (which, as some wag remarked, is composed mostly of loot). France is as greedy and apprehensive as a peasant wife with money under her petticoats, who has been robbed several times, China is a crude military dictatorship, and Russia an ironclad totalitarianism no more interested in three of the Four Freedoms than was Senator Bilbo. But neither are we wholly perfect.

What does the veteran, like the civilian, think of Russia? In 1945 one heard mostly of fraternizing on the ramparts of the Elbe; in 1946 of infiltrating spies, shootings, and kidnappings. Yet all the while a fair amount of business continues to get done despite language barriers and an atmosphere thick with suspicion. The veteran has no more infallible answer to this question than do the rest of us. He is concerned, beyond any doubt, and (as his spokesmen almost universally agree) he is no isolationist, knowing that, whether we want it so or not, responsibility for world peace rests heavily in American hands.

This is a curious situation which confronts two world powers, the United States and Russia. For generations each has thought of itself as an innocent in a wicked world—a naïve role which is no part of the national legend, for example, of Great Britain or of France. Despite proof that we have often had the best of international horse-trading—from the Revolutionary debts owed to France, to the Monroe Doctrine buttressed for a century by the British Navy, down to our indemnity for the "Alabama" claims, the shrewd purchase of Alaska, "Seward's folly," and other instances—Americans have rather consistently cherished the idea that in international affairs they are suckers and have drawn a somewhat melancholy pleasure from contemplating that fact—the majority being citizens who in their private capacity would take no pride whatever in playing such a part. I need not dwell upon this paradox in the city of Colonel McCormick.

On the other side of the hedge, czarist Russia always thought of herself as a land apart, ringed by hostile, conniving neighbors. This heritage is now doubly aggravated by the revolutionary psychology of communism, quick to regard all disagreement as depraved and sinister and armaments in others' hands as an affront to Mother Russia (who herself carries a Tommy gun in her market basket). Recent proposals of Mr. Molotov and Mr. Vishinsky that the United States call an abrupt halt to those chain reactions which began almost exactly four years ago on this campus—while they insist upon the fullest use of the veto, freedom from inspection, and refusal to bate a jot of national sovereignty—recall an incident which happened just twenty years ago, at the League of Nations Disarmament Conference in 1926. France looked with cheerful resignation upon scrapping masses of capital ships, while Britain was not loath to practice reduction of planes— with a side glance at that air armada her neighbor was supposed to be building. And then Maxim Litvinov got up and threw a mild consternation into the assembly by proposing disarmament all around. At this impasse the urbane delegate from Spain, Señor Salvador de Madariaga, took the floor and recollected an old animal fable, of how the birds of the air and the beasts of the field once met to assure the reign of peace everlasting. First, the eagle offered a resolution that teeth should be taboo; the lion declared vehemently that wings ought to be abolished. And then the bear arose and proposed that they should forget their differences and hug each other as tightly as possible.

I fancy that a good many veterans, like many citizens, are

annoyed with pressure groups' striving to impale this nation upon either of two horns—the dilemma which used to demand our choice between fascism and communism, as if there were no other destination than those twin peaks of tyranny upon either of which human liberty could just as surely founder. Now we are told to choose between Upton Close, cheap and dishonest firebrand of a new nationalist outfit called American Action, and Henry Wallace, the honest but confused liberal who is not always sure of his facts or, rather, is much too sure.

Personally, this speaker thinks (as one ignorant layman out of a hundred and forty million) that our only sensible course is to implement the excellent Baruch-Lilienthal plan for atomic control, inviting the co-operation of the world, and if Russia and her satellites accept, the cause of world peace is won; if they refuse, we and posterity will know where to place the blame.

It is safe to say that most veterans are convinced of one thing: they do not want to fight again; but, having seen the results of unreadiness and defeat in a dozen ravaged lands and between Kasserine Pass and Hurtgen Forest, having witnessed the difference between green and seasoned troops, the veteran (so far as he makes his voice heard) is no friend of sentimental, or, shall we say, penitential, disarmament. In the past, we have witnessed the folly of scrapping all military controls, of pushing the popularity of tax reduction until it endangers national safety—a danger just as real as giving over our foreign policy to the military. If we Americans, civilians and veterans, have drawn any instruction from the late struggle, surely two lessons linger: the criminal folly of aggressive war and the conviction that fearlessness for the right is a better thing than fearfulness for peace.

THE RECRUITMENT AND TRAINING OF THE NEW ARMED FORCES

HANSON W. BALDWIN

✶

THE theme of these lectures—"Civilian-Military Relationships in American Life"—reflects the somber realism of the pragmatic age in which we live. Never before in a so-called "time of peace" have Americans been so preoccupied with military problems and the details of military policy. Events of the past year unfortunately justify a cynical paraphrase of the famous dictum of Clausewitz: modern peace is an extension of war by other means.

The problem of military security is as old as the days of the club and the spear, and recruitment and training of military forces always has been a major part of that problem. But ever since the industrial revolution, and most particularly during the technological revolution which we are now experiencing, the raising of armies and navies and their training has become a more and more complex and difficult procedure.

The details of this procedure cannot be understood unless we clear away some of the trees, some of the growths of our fancy, and try to get a picture of the woods as a whole. The "recruitment and training of the new armed forces" can be discussed realistically only if the character those forces ought to assume in the atomic age is first studied.

Let us, in clearing away the trees, examine and dismiss some of the ancient, and untrue, military shibboleths.

First, dismiss the oft-repeated fallacy that we shall have "peace in our time." There is no warrant in past history or in the study of present-day man for the belief that the millennium is just around the corner. Permanent peace has been the ideal of generations, and it is still an objective devoutly to be sought. But peace is a process of education; man learns slowly, and each succeeding generation seems to forget the bitter lessons learned by the past. Permanent peace is not a certainty, not even a probability, for generations to come. Not even the atomic bomb and its terrible threat to human life and human progress will outlaw war until man learns to understand and to control himself. War, major war, will not recur tomorrow, but all the lessons of history indicate that it will probably again blight the earth before a half-century has passed.

Second, examine the assertion that we were "unprepared" for the last war and for the first World War, in fact, for all our wars. There are, and have been, of course, degrees of preparedness: before the second World War the United States had a navy equal to any and the best long-range bomber in the world; the National Guard had been federalized; and conscription had started. Nevertheless, we were "unprepared" and will always be "unprepared"; there is no such thing as absolute preparedness, and it is futile to strive for it. Germany, for instance, was prepared for the Polish campaign, but not, in any sense, for the war she got. There have been few, if any, instances in history where any nation has been completely prepared for a great war. Absolute preparedness—preparedness for any eventuality—is a will-o'-the-wisp which will lead any country which attempts it, even a totalitarian autocracy, to destruction.

Third, reject the beguiling argument that armaments mean security. Security is relative, not absolute; there is no such thing in this world in any field—labor relations, politics, economics, health—as absolute security, and it would be a dull world if there were. History shows that the greatest armaments have never meant either inviolability against attack or certainty of victory, but history does show that flabby weaknesses can invite attack. There is a happy mean in armaments as in politics.

Fourth, analyze the contentious assertion that, in case of any future war, the United States would be the first to be attacked. Unless and until some single power (other than the United States) controls all the rest of the world, that is nonsense. This same assertion—that the United States would be the first to feel the weight of any enemy assault—was made after the first World War about the second, and it was not true. Now it is being repeated. The United States may be *among* the first places attacked, but no potential enemy could neglect the danger spots nearer his borders; his first and primary objective would have to be elimination, neutralization, or conquest of our forward bases and of our allies.

Fifth, eliminate for the foreseeable future the probability of large-scale physical invasion of the United States. Invading forces can come to the United States only by sea or air, and distance and geography still have a meaning. As long as we control the sea and air, as we do today, no large-scale invasion is possible. Small-scale air-borne operations are possible; though without air superiority, very difficult. The whole history of air-borne operations shows their tremendous complexity, and the great transoceanic distances that separate us from potential enemies make any large-scale invasion through the air impossible in the immediate future and exceedingly difficult (though not impossible) in the more distant future. Massive assault rather than massive invasion is the threat to the twentieth-century United States, assault by atomic bombs, transoceanic rockets, planes, and new-type rocket-launching or plane-carrying submarines.

The woods have become a little clear, but the highroad to military progress will not be well marked unless we study the lessons of the past war.

The greatest war that history has yet recorded showed that:

1. Our educational and cultural system between the last two wars fostered a "lost generation" not mentally or spiritually prepared for war or, for that matter, for the struggles of life. Our students assimilated facts (and sometimes propaganda with the facts); but they did not learn to correlate and to analyze, and neither the home nor the school gave them faith—faith in our institutions, in our way of life, in our country. Our young men were not ready, as our enemies were, for the brutal realism of war; the "work-less-and-make-more" philosophy and the growth of urban living with its ease and comfort replaced the older and rugged virtues of the pioneer American. We taught a generation to believe that there would be no more wars; we oversimplified the causes of war into catch phrases, like "merchants of death"; we overemphasized physical freedom and personal license at the expense of spiritual duty. Hence, our young men in the last war did not believe, to the same extent as our enemies, in what they were fighting for; most of them did not know what they were fighting for. They fought to win: they fought to go home, not to make the peace.

2. Victory is no longer won by the big battalions but by the big factories. This has been increasingly true since the industrial revolution; Forrest's "to git thar fust with the most" now must be paraphrased to "git thar fust with the greatest fire power." The statistics of America's physical effort in the past war are gargantuan and unprecedented; we produced a navy and a merchant marine greater than the fleets of all the rest of the world, the greatest air force, the best-equipped army. And we shipped to our Allies the equivalent in dollar value of enough military equipment to outfit completely two thousand infantry divisions—more divisions, by far, than there were in all the world. The factories of America and the industrial know-how of America and the mechanical compe-

tence of America won the war. We must remember and emphasize and emblazon this fact upon the mind of the future: industrial strength is a major measure of national power in the modern world.

3. It takes longer to equip armies than to train them; this has been true ever since the industrial revolution. Our troops were mobilized and were training with simulated tanks, "stovepipe" mortars, and wooden machine guns months before the equipment was ready. A division can be pretty well trained, starting from scratch, in a year to fifteen months and individual replacement in less than six months; but the modern equipment required for an army cannot be produced in mass in less than eighteen months to two years. To reach full-scale industrial effort and to convert, the national economy from peace to war, two years or more are required.

4. The continental United States has become the main operating base for our armed forces, as well as the arsenal and supply base. During the war our B-29's were directed strategically and sometimes even tactically from Washington; global strategy was "made in Washington." The Navy's "floating-base" system, which used ships instead of fixed land installations to support the fleet, emphasized the importance of the main base, the United States, at the expense of fixed advance bases. This trend, in the atomic and rocket age, will become more and more pronounced; in the age of world-girdling planes and transoceanic missiles the fighting forces will operate from the continental United States.

5. The technological revolution in warfare is changing our old concepts of strategy. Missiles of supersonic speeds like the German V-2, transoceanic planes, new-type submarines, biological poisons, atomic bombs, and other new and frightful agents of destruction have conferred upon the offense a great and probably growing lead over the defense. These and other weapons—particularly the coming intercontinental and trans-

world missiles—have altered American strategical concepts. We now have for the first time in history "live" frontiers; no strength of arms, no form of defense, can guarantee America immunity against attack from rockets that move at supersonic speeds through the ionosphere or against submarines that can cross the oceans submerged to launch from beneath the sea atomic missiles against our coasts. Our "live" frontier is also the frontier of the sea, for against an enemy that moves by stealth beneath the oceans or that flies high above the waves defense is difficult. We cannot, therefore, in the future age of guided missiles and atomic explosives guarantee the reasonable security of our frontiers by defensive means. But the danger is assault and attack, not the physical invasion of large armies but assault by atomic bombs and robot death. There is no answer now foreseeable against such assault, no defense except a strong offense—the threat of retaliation in kind, the threat of worse blows against the enemy homeland than any the enemy can deliver against us. This means, strategically, that the United States must have strong offensive forces— rockets and guided missiles, long-range bombers and submarines, air-borne troops and fast, offensive naval vessels, instantly ready for *offensive* action.

6. The sequitur of this is clear: no part-time, part-trained soldiers can be instantly ready or can be expected to master the complexity of modern arms. The military forces of today must be full-time professional forces, highly trained and with healthy military reflexes.

We are thus confronted, because of the unequivocal facts of life in the atomic age, with great paradoxes which complicate the formulation of an adequate postwar military policy:

The first and greatest paradox: Offense today is by far the best defense, but how can we develop in peacetime, in a peace-loving, nonimperialist democracy, an offensive force of suitable type, ready for instant strong action? There is a psychological contradiction in these terms.

The second paradox: It is more important than ever before in history to protect the continental United States against attack in view of the tremendous importance of industrial production to modern war and in view of the development of the continental United States itself as the main operating base for our military forces. But our "live" frontiers of the air and the sea and the advantage of offensive over defensive make complete one hundred per cent "defense" impossible.

Where, then, do we stand?

Today in the great and growing struggle between extremes it is fashionable to condemn the middle-of-the-road approach. But I believe it is the only hope, the only creed for tomorrow, in military philosophy as in politics. We must support the United Nations to the maximum and create a physiological atmosphere in which this puling infant born from the loins of chaos can live and grow, even though its growth be stunted. Yet, plainly, in this era in which the physical scientists have far outstripped the social scientists, in this era of spiritual lethargy and man's distrust of man, we cannot put our dependence solely or chiefly upon the United Nations, an organization limited in its concept, circumscribed in its strength. We must still depend in major measure upon our national strength; major reduction in our military might must come only with a parallel increase in the strength of the United Nations. But we must veer neither toward military imperialism nor toward military isolationism. We must walk in military policy, as in economics and politics, the median line.

Perhaps we cannot do this; perhaps this will prove impossible in view of the unsolved and perhaps insoluble political and economic difficulties of the world. It may be beyond our skill to reconcile reasonable measures of national security with the encouragement of international growth; it may well be that compromise—the sane compromise of the middle of the road—is impossible. Perhaps history will record that Americans found that reasonable national security, based on the development of an offensive military force, was impossible without the development of American imperialism. I hope not; I believe not; but if the choice must come, I certainly prefer a world dominated by an American imperialism to one dominated by a Russian imperialism.

We can now, I think, see the woods more clearly; the character of our desirable military establishment is better defined.

1. We need primarily strong offensive forces, but not too strong, built around the new weapons: the atomic bomb (as long as it is not outlawed), long-range rockets and missiles, air power, offensive naval types, air-borne troops. Since such forces can strike at any enemy only by the seas and through the air and since the defense of this hemisphere lies in the air and at sea, not on land, our major emphasis must be on the development of air-sea weapons, of an air-sea policy, and of an air-sea strategy. There is no peacetime need for tremendous land forces in this country. Our "live" frontiers are at sea and in the air, not on land.

2. Since any forces ready for instant action and well trained in the complex modern weapons must be full-time regular forces, the emphasis must be on a professional army and navy.

3. Since many of the newest and most terrible weapons have not yet been developed to their full potential and will not be for some years and since there is no present indication that the new weapons will eliminate the need for all past weapons, we must continue—particularly in the interim future before the progeny of the technological revolution grow to maturity —to maintain and develop conventional weapons and forces: land forces, sea forces, and air forces. In other words, in the immediate future we must still depend in major measure upon the tried and trusted arms and methods that won the last

war instead of solely upon the technicians of "push-button" war. And in the more distant future we must carefully retain the efficient military means and methods of the past while simultaneously developing to the full the more terrible methods and means of tomorrow.

4. Though major emphasis must be on offensive forces, we cannot ignore defensive strength, but our defenses must be of a totally different kind and character from any developed in the past. Air and missile interception, radar, warning systems, advance bases to protect our coastlines, and active measures of defense are important; but perhaps even more so are the passive measures so strongly recommended by the Strategic Bombing Survey: disaster training, civilian defense training, anti–air-borne training, riot control, shelter construction, and decentralization of industries and of urban hospital and administrative facilities.

The size of our armed forces is best indicated by listing the tasks they may have to perform. These are occupation and policing duties in former enemy countries and such other duties as the peace treaties, the United Nations, and our foreign policy may prescribe; the garrisoning of overseas bases; the provision of a strategic reserve and training cadre in this country; and the provision of home-front forces trained and organized for passive defense.

To perform these missions, the Army has estimated that it will need a force of about 1,070,000 (including 400,000 in the Army Air Forces) as long as occupation continues, and 875,000 after occupation ends. This seems to me, at least against the vista of today, a reasonable estimate; certainly as long as our troops must patrol Germany, Austria, the Trieste area, Japan, Korea, and North China any reduction below 1,000,000 would be difficult. When occupation ends and if the world political situation has then improved, the 875,000 figure seems subject to some reduction.

The Navy has estimated its postwar needs at 552,000 officers and men, plus 108,200 marines. Control of the sea, as well as control of the air, is vital to American geographical-strategical concepts; but our Navy ended the war with no near rival, its fleets equal to all others in the world. Today there is no other great navy in the world except the British Fleet; Russia talks of naval power, but time, technique, and tradition are its main ingredients. For the immediate future, therefore, the Navy's manpower requests seem excessive; naval personnel might well be reduced to 400,000, to 300,000, or to even less; the Marine Corps to 75,000 or to 50,000.

The "civilian components," or home-front forces, organized in every state, are an important part of our postwar military establishment. The National Guard's goal has been set at 682,000 men, including twenty-seven divisions plus twelve air wings; the organized reserves contemplate a force of 874,000 men organized in twenty-five divisions in addition to many ancillary units. All the National Guard units and many of the reserves, though civilian soldiers and subject to only one armory drill a week and two weeks of active duty training each year, are classified as "M-Day" soldiers, to be ready for any form of duty anywhere in the world on Mobilization Day. These civilian components plus the Regular Army, fleshed out by additional manpower, will provide, it is contemplated, a force of 4,500,000 men for the Army in the first twelve months of any future war.

The Navy's civilian components, or organized naval reserve, to number about 200,000 in specific units, plus large unorganized forces, will also be used to fill out the crews of ships in reserve or inactive commission on the outbreak of any future war.

Such are the estimated manpower requirements of the armed services—requirements which dwarf in size all previous peacetime figures. Even if these figures can be reduced—and I have indicated that I believe that they can be by reducing the number of ships in operation, eliminating unnecessary echelons of command, and reducing the number of bases to be manned—they are still large. How can we raise such sizable forces in time of peace without the incentive of national emergency?

We have seen that our regular services must be manned by full-time, highly trained, professional soldiers, sailors, and airmen. Voluntary enlistment and preferably long-term enlistment provides the only possible answer. The part-time soldier cannot possibly be master of the intricate modern profession of arms despite all the will in the world; he cannot possibly become in his spare time, an M-Day soldier, ready for instant action. Nor will a mass-conscript army meet our needs. Not only would such an army, drawn from democratic America, where all the traditions and mores offer a psychological barrier to acceptance of conscription, suffer in morale and esprit; but, more important, it would be an inefficient army in dollars and in military know-how. The large annual turnover of a conscript army precludes continuity of training and increases expense; the soldiers are not professionals, not experts, and cannot be on any one-year conscription basis. Yet one year of service is the maximum conceivable limit which the Congress might theoretically permit in peacetime; actually, no conscription measure of any duration has much chance of legislative acceptance. Conscription, short-term enlistments, and part-time soldiers will not meet our needs.

But if this is true, what is the answer? Can we raise forces of such unprecedented size as the Army and Navy indicate are needed in this era of peril by volunteer enlistment? A year ago most Army leaders hooted at the suggestion that we might be able to raise a force of one million by enlistment. Today some of them have changed their minds. Contrary to service predictions and estimates, the Army has enlisted more than one million men, while the Navy and Marine Corps, with some six hundred thousand men in their ranks, have filled their needs completely with voluntary enlistments. Some of these enlistments were stimulated, of course, by the extension of the wartime draft act—a stimulus which cannot be depended upon after March 31, 1947, when the draft act is scheduled to expire. In major measure, however, the recruits were attracted by the high rate of pay, the opportunity for travel and foreign service, the retirement and veterans' benefits provisions, the security of a service career, educational and other opportunities, boredom with the grubbing lot of a civilian, the prospects of living better and working less than in civilian life, and the liberalization of service provisions governing the enlisted men and his relationships with his officers.

Despite these attractions the enlistment figures have been dropping during the latter part of 1946. In part this is a seasonal trend; in part it may reflect the "draft holiday" of the fall and the anticipation that the draft will end entirely in April. Economic conditions in civilian life will, of course, have much to do with the rate of enlistments; in bad times the Army and Navy never have a dearth of recruits. The forecast for the future, therefore, depends in part upon economic conditions. But in greater degree it seems to me, it depends upon reform of the personnel system in the services, in particular of the Army's system. That system came in for many just and severe criticisms during the war, for fitting round pegs into square holes, for failing to provide adequate replacements, etc. Major General Willard S. Paul, the War Department's director of personnel and administration, has admitted that "World War II certainly demonstrated our lack of intelligent personnel management," our "red tape and obsolete methods." General Paul is trying to clean up an unsavory mess, trying to put the "personal into personnel." He has a difficult job, for reforms in any military organization, bound as such organizations are by habit and tradition, are hard to effect. But reforms are being made and, if continued, the Army will offer a more attractive career. The Army is the only one of the services that has doubts about its ability to fill its needs by volunteer enlistment. The Navy and the Marines have no such doubts, and the Army Air Forces are confident that they can recruit the needed men. The ground forces suffer in appeal, as compared to these newer and more glamorous services; but proper advertisement, an increase in the incentives for long enlistments, continued liberalization and modernization of the personnel system, and perhaps some reduction in the size of the Navy will enable, I am convinced, maintenance of an army of necessary size by volunteer enlistment. If such a system fails, that failure will not be one due to falsity of a principle, for the principle of long-term professional soldiering in this atomic age is sound, but to failure of method, a lack of appeal, or an obsolescence of personnel management.

If volunteer enlistment will provide all the regular forces needed—and I am confident, given the correct management, that it will—is the Army's plan for universal military training necessary?

This plan must be distinguished from the draft act of war-time, now scheduled to expire next spring. The wartime draft act provided for the conscription for service anywhere in the world of men within a wide age bracket. The universal military training act, indorsed by the Army, contemplates the conscription annually of about 1,000,000 youths between eighteen and twenty—726,000 for the Army, between 232,000 ans 274,000 for the Navy and Marines—for training only. These lads would not be liable to service anywhere but would be assigned to special training corps with distinctive uniforms or insignia, and they would not be subject to the Articles of War but would be governed by a specially drawn code of conduct. Under present plans the youths would be given six months of training, and then, in lieu of a second six months, they would be able to enter any one of eight alternative pro-grams, including enlistment for a specified period (probably two to three years) in the National Guard, or organized reserves, enlistment in the Regular Army, etc. In other words, univer-sal military training is purely a compulsory military *training* act, which would tend to build power for the civilian com-ponents in particular and, to a lesser degree, for various ele-ments of the Regular Army.

U.M.T. promises several military advantages, and these have been so stressed by War Department spokesmen that the projected legislation has come to represent in some minds the "promised land." These advantages are principally two:

1. U.M.T. would provide a steady flow of manpower for the National Guard and organized reserves. The manpower "sights" of these civilian components have been set so high, far higher than in pre-war days, that there is considerable doubt that these organizations can recruit to full strength by volunteer enlistment, even if new inducements are provided.

2. U.M.T. would provide, in case of war, a mass of semi-trained reserves of men who had had at least some experience of military discipline and military training. This backlog of experience should shorten the period required to train a mass army after M-Day.

But the disadvantages of U.M.T. are many:

1. It would be extremely costly—probably between $1,500,-000,000 and $2,500,000,000 yearly, in addition to all other costs of the defense budget.

2. U.M.T. will require a training cadre or overhead num-bering about 132,000 regulars (for the Army alone), in addi-tion to the 1,070,000 needed for the other Army tasks already enumerated. In other words, the legislation would add to the peacetime manpower problems of the Regular Army, not sub-tract from them, for a greater number of volunteers would have to be procured.

3. U.M.T. in this atomic age promises to be of very limited military utility; the men so trained will be at best "half-baked" soldiers, and within a very few years after their release from training corps, Army, or civilian components, they would, be of very questionable value. All of them would require extensive "refresher" training after the start of any emergency; none of them (except those who stayed in the Regular Army) would be prepared to be M-Day soldiers. Much of what these men had learned four, five, or ten years before might be forgotten, might even be obsolete when war started. In other words U.M.T. does nothing whatsoever to provide highly trained units ready for any emergency when emergency comes.

4. U.M.T. would focus major attention and a major proportion of the defense dollar on producing a half-trained mass reserve force at the certain expense of more important elements of defense: research and development, tactical development, training of the regular forces, etc.

5. U.M.T., if enacted tomorrow, would disrupt temporarily the flow of students to engineering and scientific schools at a vital time when the nation, because of stupid wartime military policies, is already behind in the race of scientific education.

6. The argument can be fairly made that a far better army could be produced if it were totally trained (with the exception of the professional regular forces) under the incentive of wartime than partially trained in the doldrums of peacetime training camps.

7. Our postwar military policy as now enunciated describes the National Guard and the reserves as M-Day forces to be trained for instant duty anywhere in the world. New York State is the only state in which a State War Disaster Military Corps has been created, its primary mission that of disaster training and home-front defense. A far stronger case can be made for training the home-front civilians and the civilian com-

ponents of the services in the specialized type of disaster control, anti–air-borne work, etc., necessitated by the atomic age than for the type of training envisaged by U.M.T. Six months of routine military training is contemplated by U.M.T.—instruction in infantry, artillery, combined arms, etc.—and upon completion of this training, the trainee would pass on to more of the same in the National Guard and reserves. Therefore U.M.T. does not meet the needs of the atomic age.

8. U.M.T. will help to provide a semitrained mass army, ready long after M-Day, but such a mass army cannot ward off sudden surprise attacks by missiles or bombs. It will not implement our predominantly maritime-air strategy.

9. But perhaps the greatest disadvantage and danger of all is that U.M.T. might foster the illusion of security in public and military; it might well induce a sort of psychological Maginot Line consciousness; it would give us the shadow of security without the substance.

U.M.T. must be judged primarily on its military merits or lack of them, but I cannot leave the subject of conscription (or, called by a sweeter name, peacetime military training) without reference to its nonmilitary implications. U.M.T. in any form would affect profoundly the national society, either for better or for worse, and the whole world scene. There is not sufficient space here to discuss in detail the social, economic, psychological, and political implications of peacetime compulsory military training; but there are three major yardsticks by which the project—one which is revolutionary to American concepts and traditions—can be judged.

First, is compulsory peacetime military training an essential or highly important part of a sound American military policy?

Second, will it be for the over-all good of the nation?

Third, will it promote international understanding and peace?

The answer to all three questions, it seems to me, is in the negative.

There is one other method of recruitment for the armed forces, in addition to those previously discussed, which cannot be too lightly dismissed. Foreign legions, common in other armies of the world, have never since Revolutionary times, been an important part of American military strength. Yet, there is no reason why such units, in small numbers, should not be formed in the American Army for specialized services in certain areas of the world where no political onus would be attached to their services. The homeless Poles and other of the displaced persons of Europe—even, perhaps, a small number of the Asiatic peoples (particularly the Filipinos)—might be organized in battalions, regiments, or as a division, for service not in the political "hot spots" of the world but in Alaska and the Aleutians or in the Pacific islands. Such units should be mainly officered by Americans, and there should be at least a cadre of American noncommissioned officers. The number that could thus be employed is limited, probably no more than twenty-five thousand to fifty thousand; but careful selection and indoctrination would provide capable units. Such a plan helps to solve the services' manpower problem and has the advantage of providing the Army with men who have a tradition of professional soldiering.

The type of training which our forces need is implicit in all that has gone before. Our regular services must be highly trained, instantly ready, and tactically progressive; it will not do to learn the tactics of the next war after that war has started.

This point need not be labored long, but several important aspects of training can be summarized.

Our regular forces in this country, particularly the Army, must be kept concentrated in large camps and posts, where they will have the opportunity for large-scale maneuvers and combined training. The pre-war tendency to scatter the Army in small units at political posts all over the country is again tending to reassert itself and must be resisted. Intensive field training, directed by divisions and progressing from the school or the squad to divisional maneuvers, must be continuous. There must be far greater emphasis than ever before in the past on combined operations; land, sea, and air forces must work in close association and harmony. The task-force type of organization used during the war is needed for the immediate future and must be developed. All ground units must be capable of air-borne "lift" and trained in its tactics and logistics. Above all, the school system of the services, commendably enlarged and broadened since the war, must be emphasized; West Point and Annapolis must be broadened; and that type of "unification" which comes from within—from the mind and the heart and the spirit and from a common education—must be encouraged. A year or eighteen months of active service with each of the other two principal services (a naval officer with the Army Air Forces and ground forces; an Army officer with the Navy and Navy air arm, etc.) should be required before and officer could be promoted to the rank of colonel in the army or captain in the Navy.

The training of the civilian components—the National Guard and reserves—must emphasize far more than any present plans contemplate the home-front, disaster-control mission. The primary mission of the civilian components in this age of guided missiles and the atomic bomb ought to be not the impossible one of making full-fledged professional soldiers out of men who take one armory drill a week but defense of the home front. This is a complex and difficult task; it includes anti–air-borne training and all sorts of passive defense measures against atomic disaster, riot control, etc. Such training must also involve careful administration and detailed planning with private and governmental agencies, such as the Red

Cross, etc. The National Guard must reorient itself and prepare for the next war instead of for the past one; and it must include in its future mission the task of providing on a military basis, for no civilian defense organization can cope with the gigantic tasks of atomic disaster, the passive defense of the home front. If the Guard cannot or will not do so, a new type or organization, akin to the state guards which replaced the National Guard in the individual states during the war, must be created.

In all future training programs there must be far closer liaison between the military and the educational and industrial institutions of the country than ever before. Such liaison is essential for numerous reasons: to give the military services the full aid of the physical scientists whose discoveries will revolutionize the face of war, to give the services the breadth and benefit of the social sciences, to make military planning strictly pragmatic, to link military power to national capacity, to prevent military or mental regimentation and stagnation, and to give the coming youth a realistic but not cynical view of the world we live in. There must be no more "lost generations," nor must we bring up men meekly submissive to government and anxious only for security, even it is to be at the price of freedom.

To summarize: Our first lines of defense today in order of priority must be diplomacy to defer or limit war, a global intelligence system to give us warning of emergency, transoceanic missiles and long-range bombers, offensive naval vessels and air-borne troops, and, finally, a strong passive defense organized by the home front.

Our regular armed forces must be volunteer professionals, highly trained, excellently equipped, always ready. We must constantly remember that national power means far more than military power and that integration and proper meshing of all forms of the national effort is essential to military strength.

But our first effort in this atomic age must be political—to protract the peace, to avoid or limit war.

That, in turn, means the exercise of great care in the type of military establishment and the kind of military policy we adopt. We are walking a tightrope.

We must follow a median policy: neither an aggressive isolationism nor a so-called "defensive imperialism." We must be strong but not provocative.

Our postwar military policies—out methods of recruitment and training for the new armed forces—must be based on the stark realities of the atomic age not on outmoded concepts; but they must be built around a system of *free* men, proud of their *free* services.

CIVILIAN CONTROL OF A DEPARTMENT
OF NATIONAL DEFENSE

PAUL H. APPLEBY

✻

IT IS a common view that civilian control of the military establishment is certainly, simply, and permanently assured by provisions of our Constitution. In a still simpler way it is widely felt that the only requirement is to put a civilian at the top. Students of government understand, however, that there are real and difficult and ever changing problems in all executive control under popular responsibility and that these assume a still more serious character in civilian control of the military establishment.

The error in the simple view has now been magnified by achievement of the control of atomic energies. The great increase in the power potential of military action will tend to create a similar increase in dependence on and susceptibility to military power. There is a great tendency, of course, to create a military corner in, or to establish military dominance over, atomic power.

Recognizing that danger to civilian control of national defense is danger to democracy, we must recognize that danger to civilian control has been made enormously more critical by the new military potential. Our first task, then, is to identify important specific elements constituting danger to civilian control.

First of all must be cited a certain tendency, even in this country, to accept authority as an escape from individual and democratically organized responsibility. The tendency to

3

accept authority inevitably involves a tendency to accept or to use military authority because of its power potential and the nature of its discipline.

There is significance in the fact that when we speak of the possible arrival of a man on horseback we are thinking of a military man. When the country comes to any severe internal crisis, it is not uncommon for some conscientious citizens to give thought—even to make plans—about a military taking-over of the country to preserve order, to avert revolution, and to serve other like purposes. Alliance at such a time between the military and some important civilian segment—the reactionary, least popular-minded groups being the most probable candidates for such an alliance—would be a logical and dangerous development. Undoubtedly, because of its power and its discipline, the military establishment is a resource that must be valued for its possible usefulness in any acute crisis, domestic or international. For precisely the same reasons, because of its power and its discipline, measures are required to insure its use only in support of our social and political ideals. (In an aside it may be observed that other parts of our bureaucracy are not subject to the same kind of discipline, may not be so readily mobilized for equally unified action, and constitute no similar danger as a unified force.)

The general possibility of alliance between military and other groups, mentioned incidentally a moment ago, deserves separate emphasis. In exercising his control, the president necessarily chooses a single decision out of a variety of possible decisions on any particular matter. The tendency is for all those who favor all the other possible decisions to join in opposition to the decision he wishes to make or has made. The opposition party tends to align itself with any opposition. So do special-interest groups. In the case of military matters this means that there is an incipient opposition to any specific civilian-control decision and that opposition tends to rally around the military. The way in which some scientists have aligned themselves with the military on atomic-energy legislation is a recent case in point. The self-interest of certain communities and industries tends to throw them into constant alliance with the military group.

Another factor to be coped with exists in the tendency implicit in all organizations to confuse means with ends, to come to put growth and power of an organization ahead of the ends the organization had been designed to achieve. This tendency has a special aspect when the organization in question has high power potential and great capacity for unified action.

Another factor is found in a related tendency of parts of a large and complex organization, such as our national government, to seek autonomy from unified over-all direction. If a high degree of institutional autonomy should characterize the military establishment, the objective of popularly responsible civilian control would be lost; only by having essential controls concentrated in a politically responsible civilian department head, serving consciously as the agent of the chief executive, can control actually be exercised by the Congress and the people.

The danger to civilian control exists in a peculiar way in the military realm because of the glamour and prestige conferred by history and crisis on wearers of military uniforms. On innumerable occasions we all must have observed the vast difference in treatment accorded men wearing star-spangled collars compared with treatment of civilian officials of equal or higher status and responsibilities. Even a colonel or a major is freely given a respect sharply in contrast to the antagonistic attitude often reflected toward their civilian peers. The latter, without benefit of insignia, tend to be lumped casually and resentfully as "government clerks" and "bureaucrats." Yet it is through co-ordination of the government's civilian and military functions and concerns that the whole national interest must be served within the executive process; effective civilian top control through the president depends upon these nonmilitary officials and agencies. Thoughtless attacks upon the bureaucrats thus heighten the dangers to civilian control.

The same attitude of discrimination finds legislative expression in generally better remuneration for the military—somewhat concealed under the term "allowances," in better retirement benefits, and in other perquisites. Personal and family use of government-furnished transportation—generally withheld from civilian officials—is not an uncommon privilege for military officials. With respect to preparatory education, in-service training, and many other matters, legislation provides for military establishments administrative boons, separately considered and in practice differentiating military establishments from other parts of the government. These differences in treatment have some justification, of course. But they are not sufficiently treated in relationship to the government in general.

One aspect of this situation relates to the general administrative role of the expert. The familiar saying that the expert should be on tap, not on top, has special applicability here. The tendency to put the expert on top—always strong within specialized groups—is nowhere else so generally likely to be persuasive as when the experts are embellished with distinctive regalia and ritual. A spreading agnostic attitude seems not to attack, but even in cynicism to support, this special uniformed priesthood. Indeed, with a total absence of cynicism, we all must admit that the sociological lag behind our technological advance leaves us still rather desperately concerned about a truly adequate program of national defense. But we do believe that sheer effectiveness of military defense and assurance that the ends achieved actually will be those for which we are so desperately concerned depend alike upon our continuing ability to make military power the servant of our whole society.

Another aspect of this situation is presented by the widely held view that it is desirable to take important matters "out of politics." General uneasiness about political processes, lack of respect for politics, and inadequate understanding of the ways of democratic control reinforce the inclination to leave military matters to military experts. Yet it is prerequisite to civilian control—prerequisite to democracy itself—that political officials shall be responsible and that the political processes of democracy shall govern.

We come, thus, to the general relationship of Congress to the question of civilian control. There is in the very nature of Congress as a political and civilian body a certain basic reassurance. Yet it seems to me that two difficulties may be identified that call for vigilance. One of these is analogous to a difficulty implicit in the executive process. It exists in the necessity of dividing works into parts and of delegating responsibility. Congress faces this necessity, as does the president. Within the executive branch the consequence is that tendency to departmental and bureaucratic autonomy already mentioned. Within Congress the consequence is a tendency to committee autonomy, to subcommittee autonomy, even to an autonomy of committee and subcommittee chairmen. Within the committees special responsibilities result in members' acquiring specialized information. One is naturally inclined to be proud of and moved by that which he knows, of course, and not to be impressed equally by other special bodies of information. A member of a committee gets special attention from a department dealt with by his committee; he has his greatest influence in the executive branch over that particular department. He develops a vested interest in it and in its program because the prestige which his specialized knowledge gives him links him with the department. Congress as a whole tends to delegate to him and his fellow-committee or subcommittee members its whole responsibility. The result is that the weakest link in the chain of the congressional process in the translation of special-interest policy into total-public-interest policy. Policy here, as within the executive branch—where co-ordination is a similar weakest link—tends to be an assortment of special programs rather than an integrated and balanced program. Applied to our topic, these things mean that military and naval committees are less civilian in character and attitude than Congress as a whole and that they nevertheless tend to act in their field for the whole Congress. In such a situation, danger to adequate and constant civilian control of the military establishment exists.

The second difficulty on the congressional side exists in the separation of powers, in the consequent contest for powers between the legislative and executive branches. Just as it is conceivable that in some time of crisis a president lacking in political understanding and effectiveness might use his power as commander-in-chief in an irresponsible way, so, conceivably the Congress might at a time of executive weakness exercise control in an irresponsible way. The outstanding case in our history developed in the Johnson administration. The Tenure of Office Act provided that the president could not remove a cabinet member without senatorial approval. Another provision required the general of the armies to consider as coming from the president any instructions he received from the secretary of war, who was controllable by Congress. Unconstitutional as it surely was, this legislation remained on the statute-books for years. While the purpose was to reduce presidential powers and to increase congressional powers, the legislation could as easily have ignored the secretary of war and made the general of the armies directly controllable by Congress. This would eliminate all the values of civilian control involved in the president and the secretary of war. It would magnify the tendency to accept the "expert" point of view. It could lead to a congressional-military alliance in time of social stress, and this inevitably would present new possibilities of military domination. The point is that responsible civilian control is enhanced by maintenance of two controls—both presidential and congressional—in their respective fields.

Finally, an important impediment to civilian control of the military establishment exists in the difficulty inherent in large-scale and complex administration. This danger has been and will continue to be enhanced by the manifold developments that have made our whole society increasingly large and complex. These developments require corresponding developments in the art of complex administration. Yet that is a subject difficult to understand, lacking in dramatic quality, a dreary and drudging business. Here the point is that maintaining civilian control is more difficult, more dependent on complex processes, as our whole civilization becomes more complex.

World War II involved for some countries perhaps as much as a 70 per cent concentration of their total productive resources and impinged drastically upon their totality. No one doubts that another war would involve all societies—notably our own—still more completely. In the late thirties, when war clouds were gathering, mobilization plans developed by the military reflected some inclination to establish complete war administration under strict military control. There was at least some advance thought that activities later assigned to the War Production Board, War Manpower Commission, and some other "war agencies" should be assigned to the military. In a far more complex and exacting future situation, one may be sure that such an inclination would be stronger. The most important single decision, relevant to our topic, made during the recent war was the decision to set up civilian war agencies. Even so, of course, the question of military dominance was often raised; the wartime structure of the government was designed to raise it. This raising of issues is often an important function of structure.

While structure must, in a basic way, precede administration, it is an important element also in the actual administrative process. Administrative structure requires consideration no less than constitutional structure. The Constitution itself does provide the basic structure—not only of the entire government but also of that aspect of government we are here considering. Granted constitutional provisions making generally for a democratic, popularly controllable government; granted a structure providing for a president popularly elected and clothed with power as commander-in-chief of the Army and Navy; granted the establishment of general, fundamental controls in a popularly elected Congress—there still remains the problem of maintaining in actual performance effective civilian control of the military establishment. While it can be solved in the end only by the nation at large, the final solution is dependent in considerable part upon a contribution that must be made by public administrators; for in one important aspect the problem is a problem in public administration.

In this emphasis on the role of the public administrator there is nothing inconsistent with what already has been said about the role of experts. In the first place, proper use of civilian public administrators achieves balance as between various bodies of expert character, recognizes and utilizes more kinds of *expertise* and thus enriches the product. Further, experts in public administration at the level here contemplated are less narrowly specialized than even the highest level of military expert-administrators and therefore properly can function nearer the top. Finally, of course, professional public administrators in any case will be on tap, not on top. Political administrators and political leaders with still more general functions and responsibilities will be at higher levels. But the aspect which is least understood of the problem we are discussing is the public administration aspect. It is to this that I wish to direct attention.

Little faith should be placed in simple recipes for effective administration. Administration is complex. The "how to do it" often goes to the very heart of a program; policy and administration are inevitably intermingled. It is not popularly assumed that because a public problem is of economic character its resolution is to be left exclusively to economists. Yet everywhere there are areas where technical method and technical judgment properly have special sway. And it is recognized that the urgency of actual warfare increases the area in which decision should be left to the military. There is little danger that this area will not be sufficiently respected. Late in the recent war I heard Secretaries Stimson and Knox emphatically assure President Roosevelt that he had never invaded the technical field—and Roosevelt was as confident and competent in that field as any president we are likely to have. Indeed, as Lloyd George's memoirs make plain, the political risk of correcting the military experts is so great as to be intimidating. Since policy and administration are intermingled and policy is many times made far down the administrative line, responsible civilians should question even how a thing is to be done, for that may be of the essence of policy. Civilian control, although general, must be complete. It cannot be achieved by slogan or by fiat. It cannot exist in an administrative vacuum. The control we are discussing, then, is an aspect of the whole administrative process. It is impossible here systematically to cover that whole process. The need for popular understanding is chiefly for an understanding of things essential to the general, top civilian control for which we rely on the president and the secretary.

Let us begin with the secretary of a defense department. And let us observe at once that much of what will be said here is applicable to any governmental department; it is especially applicable to a defense department because there civilian popular control tends to be weakest.

A very large part of any administrator's function is to defend and uphold his organization to keep it strong for its designated task. He must create and maintain a climate in which the zeal and abilities of his personnel have opportunity and scope. Average administrators, including most administrators who come from another field into the leadership of a highly specialized, going organization and men who are not administrators at all in fact, do little more than this. It is not strange, therefore, that most secretaries of war and navy have been little more than civilian public advocates of the product and program of their military organizations. This would be in any case a considerable part of their responsibility.

But the responsibility of these secretaries demands more, for effective civilian control is dependent on other elements. The second important element is the very opposite of the first—the establishment of bounds for and restraints on the organization. In many administrative situations the necessary restraints against overreaching are substantially provided by the outside forces provided by competition, laws, and general social disciplines. To provide this necessary discipline is one of the functions of social organization and one of the functions of a top administrator. With respect to the Army and Navy, many of these restraints—as distinguished from the very strong military disciplines of a different sort—are relatively weak for the reasons indicated early in this discussion.

A third but similar and important element in the administrator's function is to provide a critical and imaginative climate for his organization. Reference already has been made to the tendency of an organization to confuse means with ends. With respect to the military this tendency involves danger that national defense will not be sufficiently imaginative, flexible, and dynamic; for from such confusion springs much of the tendency to follow convention, precedent, and hardened dogma. In a richly diversified society, diversified civilian activity and civilian leadership and control must provide the technology, the resource, and the stimulation increasingly necessary to a progressively more effective national defense. Instead, a military organization not critically and imaginatively led will tend simply to seek more dominance over our whole society and more funds—substituting sheer crude power for more complex and less devastating effectiveness.

In the first instance, then, the whole balance of the situation is a matter of secretarial management of a department. And the crucial fact is that no secretary can manage his department alone or exclusively through military executives. No secretary, undersecretary, and group of assistant secretaries can manage a department simply through bureau chiefs and technical staff of the same character as operating personnel. The first essential to secretarial control is that there be staff— adequate staff—exclusively serving the purposes of secretarial control. If a principal purpose of secretarial control is *civilian* control—as it is in the case of a national defense department— there must be civilian staff.

The War and Navy departments have done more than all other organizations to popularize the "staff" idea—and more to destroy it above the military level. Neither department has much truly general staff in any other than military terms. Neither has any real general staff in departmental or secretarial terms. The need must be met if we are to have effective civilian control.

The second essential to secretarial control is internal balance in structure and power. In dividing the work of a large organization, it is desirable to make the principal branches of the organization as nearly equal in size and/or importance as it is possible to do. It is desirable to assign to these principal branches functions that are competitive in terms of issues of such importance as to require top-level decision. Structure can be of such sort that top-level issues are resolved below the top

level; when this is the case, a secretary serves chiefly orna-
mental purposes. If, on the other hand, the structure is such
as to throw to the top level decisions needing attention at the
top level, if different viewpoints and interests are structurally
competitive, and if the competing lower executives are roughly equal to each other, the secretary is in a position to
compromise between the two, or between the two and proposals of his own staff; to decide in favor of one; or, with the
help of his own staff, to devise and effectuate something different from any of those possibilities. Such an arrangement gives
to a secretary a determining margin of control, and it is such
a margin on which the actuality of civilian control turns.

These two things—civilian secretarial staff and internal
structural balance—are cited as principal essentials to control
for the same reasons. The underlying needs are chiefly two: to
give to the secretary perspective on his organization and
program and to pose alternatives for decision. Truly secretarial
staff and balanced operating structure are the most useful
means for meeting these needs, and to a considerable degree
they are so mutually dependent that they can be explained
together.

Relative to a whole situation, any executive with a segmental responsibility exaggerates his segment; his attention
and interest are concentrated upon it. He makes correspond-
ingly exaggerated recommendations. He can most happily
accept reductions or co-ordinating modifications from his
chief when he actually sees his chief subjected to competitive
forces. The word "forces" is intentional; a sincere and zealous
lower executive is less likely to be impressed by a competing
point of view than he is by a competing force. He is most
amenable when he can say to himself: "The Chief would have
gone along with me on merit, but he had to make concessions
to these other people." As for the principal executive, unless
he is confronted with competing forces, he has little oppor-

tunity to see alternatives and little power to do anything but approve one segmental recommendation after another. Yet a good administrative whole definitely is not the sum of these segmental parts; if it were, our ideal of a good administrator would be a power-driven cigar-store Indian, with a rubber stamp in lieu of tomahawk.

Nor can a good administrator be merely an umpire. He must be a force, too. And he cannot be much of a force without the systematic help of a staff whose whole excuse for being is in the secretary's function, a staff looking at the secretary's whole responsibility as systematically as operating units regard their segments. Competing operating units and secretarial staff provide three-dimensional perspective for the intradepartmental job.

Of course, anyone who ever has served as secretary of a national defense establishment will insist that he has had to deal with an ample number of competitive intradepartmental difficulties. But these too frequently are technical differences, segmental prerogative differences, and umpire references. Too *in*frequently are they matters involving real program control and leadership control; too infrequently are they matters that involve restraints against overreaching; too infrequently do they involve development of a more critical, more imaginative, climate. And these are the things essential to true secretarial control and to civilian control.

It has been suggested that the Army and Navy have tended to make their own staffs cover the field of the secretarial staffs, thus doing violence to the reality of the staff idea. It was not intended to suggest that this encroachment was conscious and vicious. The military staffs moved into an administrative vacuum and generally with full co-operation of the respective secretaries. The result has been that in each department nearly all the basic authorities and controls have been vested in one military administrator, remaining only morally and in a certain public-relations way vested in the secretary. In the Navy it was until recently the commander-in-chief of the fleet and chief of naval operations; in the War Department it is the chief of staff. It would be difficult indeed for the kind of competitive recommendations I have had in mind to move to and beyond this officer to the secretary and extremely difficult for a secretary to give to the organization so formed the kind of critical and imaginative leadership I have been advocating. In addition, there is little place where collateral stimulation can originate. Such a structure can provide a secretary with little managerial perspective and little dynamic material. It is not intended to suggest that in practice civilian control already has been abandoned or that present secretaries do not exert considerable power. It is intended to say that political morality is now the chief citadel of civilian intradepartmental control; a good deal of that morality has been possessed by both secretarial and military personalities. Indeed, it should be noted here that the nation is enormously indebted to some of the military leaders of this period for their intelligent devotion to democratic ideals. Speaking from personal experience, I can cite particularly General Marshall, General Eisenhower, and Admiral Nimitz. For example, I have heard Admiral Nimitz say that the joint chiefs of staff should have nothing to do with budgeting but should do technically military programming. In general, the professional military men in America are much more aware of the proper limitations of their roles than are reservists, temporary officers, and many citizens.

Nevertheless, institutions should not be so largely dependent upon qualifications of individuals. The present situation is not nearly well enough supported by administrative structure and facilities.

Hence it is an important, if mild, statement that Dr. Troyer S. Anderson, historian of the Office of the Undersecretary of

War, made in a recent book review in *Military Affairs*. He said that we are generally not aware of the "influence upon the Navy Department—and the same factor is apparent in the War Department—of the absence in this country of an adequate body of top-level civil servants."

It would be possible to go on in some detail to a discussion of the structure and comprehensive functioning of a truly secretarial staff and particularly to emphasize among other things the importance of an adequate departmental civilian budget office, an adequate departmental civilian personnel office, and departmental civilian research and program-planning units and to talk about the plight of a civilian staff surrounded by operators in uniforms. It seems desirable here, however, to deal more broadly with the subject.

But even the broadest approach requires consideration of education and other preparation for high posts, both military and civilian.

The task of military leaders, even within the bounds here suggested, has been so broadened and complicated as to raise the most insistent questions about the conventional education that remains the means of providing the principal military leaders. Its narrowness makes both for administrative inadequacy and for an increase in stresses between military and civilian elements. Here, surely, is a place where civilian statesmen, educators, and administrators can make an important contribution.

Similarly, the tasks of civilian public administrators and officials have been broadened and complicated. There is a general shortage of persons even fairly well qualified to administer organizations so large, complicated, and socially significant as our military establishment. There is a general shortage of *national* political leaders. There is a general shortage of top-level administrative civil servants. There is more inclination to make provision for top-level specialists than there is to provide for top-level generalists. And we still know far too little about the best educational preparation for such persons. Our whole educational effort is designed to produce specialists and individualists rather than to produce generalists who understand and can act and support action in intricate organized efforts. The secretary of a national defense establishment should be very conscious of these needs. If he is conscious of these needs, he will fill them in some degree, somehow or other, and will not be completely overpowered by the specialists around him. But civilians who are concerned about civilian control must be concerned, too, about public administration, education for public administration, and in-service development of public administrators. The whole government should carry on systematic search for and development of adequate administrative personnel.

If there are proper intradepartmental arrangements of the sort here suggested, the possibility of actual civilian control will be much advanced. A considerable part of the gain will be an increase in the department's susceptibility to presidential control. It is to that crucial aspect of our subject that we need now to turn.

The situation of the president is similar to and yet different from that of a secretary of a national defense department.

It is similar because both are heads of large organizations. It is dissimilar because the secretary's organization—big and complex as it is—is narrower, more highly specialized, more highly integrated in the same sense that it is specialized, and peculiarly disciplined in its specialized interest. ("Integrated" and "disciplined" are terms applying below the secretary's level, if not on it.)

The two situations are similar in the fact that in both cases control can be certain only if there is a balanced organizational structure supporting top control and if there is adequate staff serving that control. They are dissimilar in the fact that the president's control is to a large extent dependent on the reality of the secretary's control, whereas as a general thing the secretary need have little doubt about the reality of the control of his line officers. They are dissimilar in the fact that in large organizations the higher the level of control, the more difficult is the actuality of control; the two situations are markedly different in levels.

This difference in levels is pervasive. While the president's function, like that of the secretary, involves his defense of his organization, the scope and character of the president's organization are to be sharply differentiated from the scope and character of the secretary's organization. In the case of the president his organization is the whole government, and the whole government is generally representative of the whole society. The president's basic organizational responsibility tends, therefore, all other factors being neutral, in the direction of all that is suggested by the phrase "civilian control." That all other factors are not neutral was the point of the first section of this paper.

Actually, the two organizational responsibilities—those of the president and those of the secretary of a national defense establishment—are to a considerable extent hostile. Everything that has been said about the secretary's total responsibility and the segmental responsibilities of his executives applies here with enhanced force. The president has to embody the whole public interest and every public interest, has to resolve conflicts involving every public interest, has to be sensitive to more than all the departments and agencies put together, has to synthesize program and action in terms of the sensibilities, hopes, and needs of the infinitely complex society that is America. What he does can not be simply the total of what his subordinates do and propose. It is this situation that has led one of the profoundest observers of our government to say privately that the cabinet members are the president's worst enemies. In only a sense is this true, but it is true enough to point to a very serious general problem of government. That problem is most serious as it involves the president's ability to control the military establishment.

If the president is not simply to ratify proposals from the military establishment, then, his basic needs are three: first, a secretary or secretaries who can in fact control the establishment for the president, who recognize their role as presidential agents, and who consistently try imaginatively to serve as far as they can his broadest responsibilities; second, adequate staff systematically working in the president's interest; third, a structural balance in the executive branch making for controllability. Here, as at the secretary's level, the purpose is to provide perspective, to pose alternatives, and to put the president in a position to wield in fact a balance of power. Mere authority without these things is generally meaningless.

At the secretary's level the same needs are so technical and so removed from public gaze that they will perhaps never be widely or well understood. At the presidential level they are of such tremendous importance that they require public understanding and so exposed to view that it is reasonable to hope that they will be understood. At this level, therefore, we should consider separately and in some detail the matters of structural balance and staff.

One purpose of structural balance is to enable an executive to delegate powers somewhat evenly and, consequently, to retain powers of about the same order of importance—thus to keep all parts of his organization under about the same degree of control. Actually, however, organizational activities differ in kind and change in administrative or policy importance. Hence, this kind of balance cannot be maintained in a changing situation. It is not even desirable that it be fully maintained, because less constant control of conventional and routine operations frees an executive to give closer attention to highly important, difficult, and controversial business.

Therefore it is not the kind of balance that makes for about the same degree of control over all parts of an organization that here is being emphasized. Rather, it is a balance that relates to the handling of the more important, difficult, and controversial business. Almost by definition, this kind of business is emergent, changeable, unpredictable. A structure laid down in law is not at all likely to provide administrative balance in these terms. In normal times no consistent insight into the problems of national defense can be expected by the president from the competing or collateral functional learning of the postmaster-general, the heads of the Federal Works Agency, Federal Security Agency, National Housing Authority, the Home Owners Loan Corporation, or the secretary of the Treasury, although all these customarily sit in the cabinet. Little more can be expected, for this purpose, from the attorney-general, or the heads of dozens of commissions and independent offices that report to the president. A rather vague functional interest and occasional bits of information might be expected from the secretaries of agriculture, interior, labor, and commerce, but it would not weigh much in these particular scales. To ponder such a situation is to marvel at the administrative illiteracy of those who talk about achieving "cabinet government" at any president's casual behest. The cabinet structure does not give the kind of structural balance we here are seeking. Even the State Department gives no consistent and comprehensive attention to the business of relating its functions and the national defense function. Aside from a general competitive attitude toward apportionments of the budgetary total, the national defense establishment normally is pretty completely isolated from the rest of the government. This puts the president in a position of weakness; he is unarmed by systematic competitive and complementary information insistently urged on him by competitors of the military; in critical and skeptical attitudes toward the military he is unsupported by powerful competing elements in his own organization; he is without organizational resources to devise imaginative counterproposals when the military come forward with enlarged demands of traditional sort.

The kind of structural balance the president needs, if he is to effect real civilian control, must be administratively devised and administratively maintained.

There appear to be three principal possibilities which together could provide the desired administrative structural situation. The first of these is to develop the relevant functions of the State Department and thus to strengthen its position and voice in councils dealing with defense. That is the one department with responsibilities and outlook directly bearing on those of the defense establishment. Yet it has been said, and probably with substantial truth, that the State Department has not nearly often enough opposed a military proposal and often has simply supported military demands. An outstanding exception has been the undeniable fact that the State Department has strongly influenced—even on occasion determined—military policy behind our advancing troops. The further the military advance, the stronger has been the State Department influence, until it has come to its peak in postwar occupation. This is a proper progression. But the very insufficient State Department participation in and influence on the defense program in peace and in early stages of war impairs our policy and endangers civilian control. To much too great an extent the military departments make and act on their own interpretations of the international political scene.

Assumption by the State Department of a major reponsibility for intelligence is a principal need. A part of the intelligence function has a technically military character, but most of the intelligence function has a civilian-political character, and the over-all appraisal of intelligence is properly a civilian-political function. If the management of intelligence is left to the military—as it is for the most part, in spite of contrary occasional stimulation—elements of civilian control are left in the weak position of confronting organized information with—at best—piety.

Beyond this the State Department needs to maintain a day-to-day systematic working relationship with the defense establishment that will put it in a position to have an informed and penetrating judgment of the whole defense program. This it does not have.

Finally, in this field as in others, the State Department has a newly great responsibility for focusing on international policy the whole of our domestic policy and for focusing on our domestic policy the new requirements of international collaboration and national action abroad. In other words, in terms of our topic, the State Department alone can be looked to, to bring to bear on our national defense program the competitive and varied all-government, total public policy—interests whose relationship to defense otherwise will be but dimly recognized. Labor, agriculture, finance, commerce, and welfare considerations are in actuality deeply and increasingly involved in defense programs. Our economy and our social order are deeply involved.

Nothing here said is intended to reflect on either the military or the State Department. The military, as any other specialized interest, will be as aware of considerations outside its special field as social and administrative forces require it to be. And the responsibilities of the State Department have been both so magnified and so multiplied as to leave it staggering under the load. Yet acknowledgment of responsibility is the first step toward fulfilment.

The second principal possibility for providing structural balance is in peacetime to maintain and keep active in civilian hands certain embryonic civilian war agencies. The most important of these would have the function of planning mobilization—which covers in a planning sense the entire area of war administration. Auxiliary to this should be the function of stock-piling strategic materials—now under the Army-Navy Munitions Board. Possession of an operating function of that kind is one of the best ways to insure active life for the group charged with preparations for mobilization. Military relationships with civilian atomic-energy control probably should be bridged in part through the mobilization unit, too—not through military membership on the Atomic Energy Control Commission.

The third principal possibility for providing structural balance is in the management of certain aspects of military and military-related research. Strictly operational research properly and most effectively can be carried on within the military establishment. But broader and more imaginary research with defense significance should be carried on not in isolation from the military but under separate responsibility. The same responsibility should cover some of the important relationships between civilian atomic-energy control and the military. From the research unit should come much of the needed stimulation to adopt new and more effective defense methods and devices.

The question of whether a single department of defense makes for greater or less structural balance and consequent controllability also requires consideration. It cannot be covered here.

It would be impossible here to discuss comprehensively the subject of presidential-staff assistance. Yet, because provision of staff service in the interest of civilian control of the military establishment must fit into the general presidential situation, a few observations are offered.

In one aspect nothing is more important to a president than

staff in whose personal loyalty he has the highest confidence. This means the president must have complete freedom in the selection of his top staff.

In another aspect nothing is more important to the president than staff widely experienced in governmental operations. This means that to an important degree top-staff persons should be career or semicareer government people.

In still another aspect the most important requirement is that staff members serving at the apex of the executive government should have the very broadest comprehensions and the very extraordinary abilities that contribute to the integration of manifold, diverse, and far-flung activities into a pattern of policy, program, and administration that makes sense as a whole. The president's function is government-wide, society-wide; those who intimately serve his function should have and be capable of performing government-wide functions, even though from special vantage points. They should not be technicians or have too specialized assignments; necessary staff functions of specialized sort should be performed below them.

These three rather contradictory requirements have to be reconciled and related to some additional, minor requirements: staff arrangements must be flexible and yet contribute an institutional character to the presidential office, for example.

One specific point especially relevant to our topic stands out from the foregoing description of staff needs. This is that military aides should not have staff status. Indeed, the point may be stated more generally: No staff aide reporting directly to the president should have any regular assignment coextensive with a single department or any two departments. A corollary is that at the president's level, even more certainly than at the secretary's level, the general staff should be a civilian staff with no special vested interest in military affairs. In ordinary matters at ordinary times the military general staff should function within the defense establishment. Extraordinary matters and situations do require variation from this pattern, and the consequent tendency is to make a constant and basic deviation after the emergency. This deviation, in turn, is increased in abnormal times, leading to still further deviation in normal times. It cannot be emphasized too much, therefore, that even in time of war, the military general staff should be confronted with and balanced by an adequate general staff of civilian character. In the recent war Harry Hopkins served to some extent in this fashion. In so doing, however, he was merely an individual—an influential individual, but one not possessing the resources of information and systematic review that a staff organized behind him would have conferred upon him.

Presidential staff, therefore, is of two main varieties: individuals serving the president in an intimate, personal way and organized units whose chiefs combine an intimate relationship with leadership over systematic staff functions. The two varieties must be knit together, but both are needed.

The oldest organized staff unit serving the president is the Budget Bureau. It is one of two arising from permanent legislation. The others now existing are the Office of War Mobilization and Reconversion and the Council of Economic Advisers. The name of the former indicates its temporary nature as now constituted. The second is just now in the stage of initial organization.

While the Economic Council may come to exert some general, indirect influence on the military program, it has not been conceived as in any sense a civilian unit exercising "control" of the military establishment. Discussion of the council, therefore, can be dismissed here as irrelevant to our topic except for its identification with the future presidential staff which must be generally organized to meet all presidential needs, including his needs as commander-in-chief of the Army and Navy.

During the war the Office of War Mobilization performed an important, though not consistent, function in reconciling activities of war agencies. As, in keeping with its change in name, its emphasis shifted to reconversion activities, its bearing on the military establishment was sharply diminished. It seems doubtful whether in the future it or its successors will have any consistent and special responsibility contributing to civilian control of the military establishment. That remains a general responsibility of the general presidential staff.

Of the general presidential staff, the largest organization, the one with the longest history, and the one with the most systematic function bearing upon the whole executive government is the Bureau of the Budget. There review of all programs, organizations, and activities, civilian and military, is carried on regularly; there an effort toward reconciliation, balance, and integration is implicit and continuing. Its functions, however, are and should be limited.

Whatever the Budget Bureau does is limited, first of all, by its staff character. It cannot and should not determine the size of the Army, the size of the Navy, the size of the occupation forces, the policies of occupation forces, the officers to be promoted, departmental organization, governmental organization, executive office organization, or any of a great number of other things, all having an important bearing on our topic. In so far as these things are to be determined within the executive branch, they should be determined by the president, by the secretaries, by the president and the secretaries, by the president and the secretaries with the help of their respective staffs, by the executive branch generally, and in the light of congressional attitudes and consultations.

Whatever the Budget Bureau does is limited in another aspect by its special functions. Budgetary review does involve some review of policy and considerable review of administration, but in both respects there is a specialized slant that makes the review very substantially less than total review. From a special vantage point the bureau exercises an important influence on the totality, contributing to control, yet distinctly and properly remaining less than control.

The scope of the Budget Bureau's function relative to our topic probably should not be expanded, although areas within its present scope should be covered more intensively. Even then, as now, the knowledge and understanding of bureau staff relevant to civilian control will be insufficiently appreciated, and the bureau's influence on control will be less than the importance of civilian control warrants. It should be worth while to emphasize the validity of the budgetary approach to control even while recognizing its limitations.

Within military departments, as within all others, the budgetary process is a basic element of the administrative process. In all the departments the budgetary process has many identical and many similar factors. Through it, program is developed and translated into terms of personnel, plant, supplies, activities, and money. Through it, money determinations in terms of appropriations are translated into obligations and into expenditures, in terms of personnel, plant, supplies, and activities. The process requires and reflects program planning developed on paper by means of assumptions and calculations. Budget Bureau staff, observing and reviewing this process in all departments and agencies, develops a special competence in it and a special insight into it. Staff members are enabled thereby to challenge methods by which calculations have been carried on, to a point giving them considerable mastery of the departmental budgetary job. Hundreds of times a year they make calculations of their own that eventually are accepted by the agencies. Less often, but still frequently, they are able to challenge assumptions underlying calculations. And by branch and field studies they are able to put many departmental reports to the test of review of performance. In the whole process they get judgments about the kind of administrative job that is being done and about its strong and weak points. Dozens of times during the war the defense establishments called on bureau staff members for particular studies and recommendations and later awarded to these staff members citations attesting to their contributions.

In spite of all this, the public has had a chance to observe within the last year a tendency to look upon the budgetary review as a wholly incompetent interference with military experts. A reasonable and more than ordinarily careful Washington newspaper last winter flamboyantly attacked as the product of a "bookkeeper's pencil" the president's estimate of $4,148,409,300 new appropriations for the Navy Department for the fiscal year 1947. At that time spokesmen for the Navy Department flatly advocated before congressional committees about two billions more than the president's estimate. The naval committees of Congress explosively attacked the estimate. The issue of civilian control of the military program thus has been publicly posed in the present postwar year, the argument seeming to be that the president and his "bookkeeper" budgeteers should not question the program requests of the admirals. In this particular case the admirals lost the argument; talk of congressional investigation quickly subsided; and the actual authority to obligate given by Congress to the Navy differed from the president's estimate by only $43,294,000, or 1 per cent. It is doubtful, however, whether the argument was settled on merit; the general desire to reduce governmental expenditures probably was determining.

The Budget Bureau should be subject to attack, of course. So should the president's estimates. But the facts that the president is a civilian and that the Budget Bureau is a civilian agency should not be the justification for the attack. Nor should it be assumed that because there are areas of military expertness the whole military field is one in which only military expertness is relevant.

At the present time, as in the past, the Budget Bureau is the only organization giving systematic civilian review to military programming, administration, and operation. For the rest, presidential-staff review is on an individual and intermittent basis. The strengthening of the whole executive office staff and its better organization to make for balance, integration, and control of the executive government is the greatest single need in the field of public administration in America. It is a special and most difficult subject that here can only be cited as requiring a great deal of attention if we are to have confidence in the maintenance of civilian control of the military establishment.

This discussion, even in the general terms here attempted, would be incomplete without pointing to the matter of personal qualifications desirable in civilian officials responsible for military control. If we can finally establish safeguarding structure and institutional facilities favorable to civilian control, then—but only then—will the range of deviation somewhat safely turn on individual performance in key positions.

To begin with, emphasis on the importance of the role of political officers should be renewed. The American public too much distrusts politics and political officers. Yet it is only through politics and political officers that civilian control can be exercised. Those of us who are especially interested in public administration are inclined to fall into an error similar to that of the popular prejudice. We define public administration at too low a level. We tend to rate as a good administrator one technically competent and at best aware of the need to be responsive to political officers. We need more often to think of a good public administrator as one especially able to lead an organization in terms of the internal and external forces that bear on it—in other words, as one able to deal with great social forces and through his leadership to relate his organization to the social scene. The first requirement for individuals in the key posts we are discussing, then, is broad judgment, broad understanding of America and America's place in the world. An internationalist point of view as distinguished from a nationalist point of view is increasingly imperative.

Only secondarily should we consider the very real problem of amateurishness in our public officials. The nation has pathetic facilities for developing a sufficient pool of national political figures actually prepared for high-executive or general-staff posts.

A third guide has the value of mathematical probability, even though rare individuals might be exceptions. The general rule surely should be to avoid putting professional military men in high political offices. On a lower level, the same considerations would argue against using vividly successful military field commanders in general-staff positions, where the requirements are widely different.

Finally, of course, there is the question of political philosophy held by individuals concerned. Devotion to popular government must be held deeply and illumined with understanding.

If the people of America are sufficiently aware of the fact that civilian control is never finally achieved but poses a continuing problem requiring constant watchfulness, our leaders will be better suited to their roles and our institutions will be strengthened in the way of popular government.

GOVERNMENT OF CONQUERED AND DEPENDENT AREAS

T. V. SMITH

✻

THE occasion permits two introductory remarks about military government, i.e., the government by soldiers of civilians in conquered territory. The first is that the United States has had more experience at the business than is commonly recognized. It comes indeed as a surprise to some students and as a shock to most citizens that, in a relatively brief and putatively unwarlike history, the United States has engaged in some two dozen enterprises in which the military was for a season made supreme over civil authority. The second World War was, however, the first of the many occasions in which we prepared in advance for the task, recruiting specialist personnel, training men not only in the military but also in the language, culture, and governments of the lands to be conquered, and according them a functional status worthy of their civil attainments and honorable to their military vocation.

The second remark, surprising to some, though truistic enough in itself, is that *military* government is *government* nevertheless—government with all the perplexities swollen enormously and the rewards diminished abominably for a people with democratic aspirations. Can anything be more contradictory, for instance, to the genius of democracy than a government in which—and this is the official, the *Manual* conception of military government—*all power*, executive, judicial, and legislative, is put into the hands of one man?

There are two further observations that bear initial remark about military government. Any government, even civil government is mostly a continuing choice between evils; and military government is a harsh choice between colossal evils. Swell the ordinary difficulties of ordinary government—which everybody criticizes and which few find virtuous enough for the tiniest praise—swell these by a thousand; and you will have military government. This means that one is wise to count moderate failure as high success. The other observation is that, notwithstanding, military government is also government by public opinion. No people can for long be governed against its will. At the best the consent is glad, as in early days after the conquest of Italy and as, externally at least, it continues to be in Japan. At the worst military rule rests upon a consent in which hope as motive is minimized and fear maximized. But it involves consent or it soon ceases to be government.

In Sicily I turned over my own office and an adequate part of our educational building at Palermo for two weeks in order to train Sicilians in the art of taking a sort of Gallup poll of Sicilian public opinion. Later in Italy I had to reinforce from headquarters this role of consent upon a trigger-happy American provincial governor. He had complained bitterly that he could get nothing done in his province because, as he put it, I would not talk big, as he said he did, to the Italian minister whom I controlled. I tried to remind him of political realities in form laconic: "When I have the power," I wrote him in two lines, "I needn't talk big; and when I haven't, I dasent."

Such mistakes at the peripheries of power were the opposite, however, of the mistake I think we often made at the center of our late efforts at military government. Of my two chief criticisms of our military government in general, the first is that we paid too much attention to public opinion, especially to public opinion back home. Our civil experience has sensi-

tized us to this, and I suspect we overdid it in military government. It is a wry criticism for a democrat to make; for surely
the democrat must approve as well as applaud the role of public opinion in all things political. The democrat needs, however, the insight of the republican. And that is that, while
good government hears public opinion, the best government
does not respond to it neatly. To jump too quickly in response
to popular outcry is to be caught in the toils of public opinion
on the rebound, and this is to become discontinuous in policy,
the chief enemy to the legitimacy of rulership, whether in civil
or in military guise. Only steady opinion should count in
governing; and it is indeed part of the business of governing
to help steady opinion by standing firm against opinion until
it is seasoned through initial reluctance of representatives to
obey it.

It was our trigger-happy response to public opinion, both at
home and in the field, which largely accounts for what, in my
opinion, is the worst mistake we have made in military government in any of the conquered countries. I refer to the mistake we have made in Germany in regard to political purification, "denazification" as we call it. Since in a democracy what
men think, if they merely think it, is nobody's business,
ideological purification is deeply contradictory to the genius
of our free system. Still, since an ideological war was forced
upon us, we had to do something about psychological poison
once victory was won, and this in all three of our major
conquests.

In Italy we balanced the claims of civic efficiency with those
of political purity and made only a down payment upon
"epuration." We did little enough so that what we did,
stayed done, for the most part. The same goes for Japan. In
Italy we averaged less than 5 per cent removed from teaching
posts, and in Japan we have removed so far only about 2 per
cent. But in Germany public opinion blew the block when the

concentration-camp atrocities were fully exposed. We undertook to purge, on ideological grounds, more than half of all
the teachers in our American Zone.

Now I do not object to what we did, not on any pure moral
grounds. Where everybody is more or less guilty, everybody
might on a priori grounds be properly purged. There are no
purely ethical considerations which enable us to strike a balance between the necessity of carrying on and the rightful demands for getting rid of scoundrels. What one cannot achieve
of insight through the front door, however, may be discovered through the back door. Continuity of policy, as I have
suggested, is a deep, perhaps the deepest, element in the
legitimacy of any governing group. Men need so poignantly to
know in advance what they can realistically hope and what
they must prudently fear that they grow discouraged at a
policy that is discontinuous and lose respect for those who are
responsible for the uncertainty.

In Germany, for instance, we fired more than half of all
teachers. But the schools which, for various reasons, had to
be kept going have been and are kept going only in name.
Through a law which we helped the Germans formulate the
judicial process of rectification of our recklessness is now
putting back into office three-fourths or more of those we
fired. The schools lost their needed services meantime; aggres-
sions were bred in those thus set aside; and complete forfeit
was made of the element of compassion, which we permit the
German authorities to exploit when we might have turned
that exploitation to the protection of our own legitimacy.

To have so large a proportion of those "purified" by us now
thrown back into our face while we are still more or less in
command of the field seems to argue either that we were too
ignorant to know what we were about or too weak to see our
policy through. Neither lack of insight nor lack of stamina
is a good foundation for the legitimacy of any governing

group. Through such consideration of the necessity of continuity in the morale of rule we come, roundabout, to the conclusion that as a policy, even in the matter of purification, it is
better to bite off only what we can chew and then to chew it.
In Germany we have bitten off ten times more than we are
chewing, and the regurgitation is foul in our own face. The
present threat to take back the power is in for hard sledding
whether we go through with it in sixty days or not.

It is difficult, however, to emphasize too much this error
in *military* government without castigating the growing
weakness of democratic government throughout the world: a
premature sensitivity to public opinion rather than a seasoned
stamina in standing ground against public outcry until it
settles down to a demand which will sustain efforts to implement itself. That is another story, a larger and longer story,
but a story which does not belong here.

Passing up such over-all criticisms, then, let us now aim
at centrality in evaluation of our military government in
recently conquered lands. Accepting the contradiction of
democratic genius implied by war and involved in government
by the military, let us judge our performance in all these
lands against our national ideological commitments.

These major commitments, at the constitutional level, are
threefold, and all three are all against military occupations
and what such occupations historically stand for. The first of
these is indeed the categorical prescription that in just government the military shall always be subordinate to the civil. The
second doctrine—the separation of church and state—rein-
forces philosophically the foregoing political point; for, being
interpreted, this separation seeks to rule out of moral account
both the tyrannical will to power of political sinners and the
fanatical will to power of sinful saints. The third doctrine—
supremacy of the judicial in the inevitable family competition
among departments for primacy—but writes large the moral of

the other two: that he who is least powerful should become the most influential, high servant of all.

Since the occasions for our present government of occupied territories are one and all ideological, it would seem reasonable to suppose that our over-policy would be directed to ideological ends; and if to any ends, why not to this trinity of ends that inform our own constitutional enterprise? It is inevitable that we serve ends, whether we avow them or not; and it is equally foregone that our performance will be judged by others against the ideals of collective life which our culture enshrines. If we were like our nearest competitor in power—the Soviet Union—we would, like her, drive hard to duplicate in conquered territories the institutions which we have built and which we revere at home. We are, however, not like our competitor, not in methods at least. We cannot duplicate, because we believe in variety. We have to permit, and in the end to approve, multiplication, not mere subtraction or even division. Since, though our approach differs, we wish others to enjoy the ends of freedom which we ourselves revere as an ideal, it will be a convenient framework for our major discussion, a discussion unwieldy because morally ambiguous and world-wide in scope, if we make our three main constitutional doctrines the criteria by whose prosperity and spread to assess our far-flung efforts at military government. The paradoxical nature of our situation and the spirit of our enterprise are illustrated by the opening remarks of the Japanese Minister of Education, addressed in 1946 to the United States Education Mission to Japan:

We Japanese [he said in substance] may find it difficult to be model conquered people, seeing that for some two thousand years of our national history we have never been conquered before. But our intentions to that end are honorable, and we shall do our best to be model conquered people. Do you but kindly coach us if you see us falling short.

On the other hand [he continued], I surmise that you Americans are not without embarrassment. You may find it difficult to be a model conquering people, seeing that in your one hundred and fifty-odd years of national history you have not been in the habit of conquering other peoples. I know that your intentions are honor-able, and I do not fear that you will make the mistake that we Japanese made in the heyday of conquest, that of trying bodily to inflict our way of life upon the conquered. But with your youth, energy, and efficiency you may well be tempted to set a pace which we Japanese, with all honorable intentions, cannot maintain. Do you let us coach you if we see you making this mistake. With such honest endeavors on both sides, each helping the other to avoid mistakes, we may yet demonstrate to the world a model relationship between honorable conquerors and those honorably conquered.

The Japanese minister's is a proper note of modesty and mutuality for us to strike as we approach now a subject too much for any one military governor and much too much for one who at best presumes to be but "an ignorant man and philosopher." Though I have been exposed to all the major conquered peoples, I have only two eyes, two ears, and have had but a limited time to profit from the experiences of others and to come to understand the half of what I know. A decade hence we shall have begun to pool and digest our experiences and perhaps to achieve a reasonable perspective upon our per-formances. Premature assessments, like this one, may, how-ever, prove worth while if approached in the spirit of one who knows that he is not God. It is testimonial to my fear that I shall be found outtalking my information, as I shall certainly exceed my wisdom, that I organize what more I have to say around the fate under military uniforms of our three major constitutional doctrines, doctrines inherited by us from Fathers who were wise well beyond their time.

How, then, stands American military government when judged by our first constitutional canon, that the military shall be subordinate to the civil? Though the very fact denies the ideal, the question is nevertheless worth asking. The answer is indeed reassuring. Bluntly, our military government stands justified by this very standard: we Americans are determined to subordinate the military even if we have to use the military to do it! Nor is this a mere contradiction of the sheerly logical; it is the law of collective life, which knows no logic save that spelled our in the dynamic evolution of the better from the worse. Power-to-perfect has always been required to cope with the power which precedes and circumvents the advent of any ideal. That fact we were by way of forgetting when we were goaded out of our latent (military) weakness into a superlative martial effort to save our and the world's freedom. Those destined by tyrants to die by the sword must take up the sword in order to live, if possible, and, if not possible to live, to die honorably. We have had to become stronger than we like in order to defeat an arrogance of strength which we hate. Having defeated it, there was nothing to do but take over and use our own strength to dissipate its arrogance. We were driven to war and have inherited military government at all only because of the previous supremacy in these now conquered lands of the military over *their* civil authority. We shall be judged by our constitutional conduct, not by the historic contradiction of our constitutional conscience, into which we were forced. Others will judge us as we now judge ourselves, in terms of the use we make of our opportunity, as option returns to our hands by the strength of our arms. The key to the verdict is found in this: that a military which is civil in intent is by no means militaristic in tendency.

Utilizing that key, this story emerges from our occupation of conquered lands: a common policy in all of them of withering our military away as rapidly as their civil can be reinstated. In Italy the Germans had hardly been driven from the "ankle" until we were "turning over" to an Italian civil government, restored and defascistized (which meant at least demilitarized) all the fuctions of government it could possibly handle. In truth the poor Italians had hardly got comfortable to be governed (my own minister of education had not so much as a typewriter to his name!) until we were asking them to govern themselves. "You'll learn to do," we said to them, "only by doing!" We constantly pushed the Italians into civil initiative by giving them a responsibility they were most reluctant to accept. We aided their efforts, without ourselves taking credit for the results; we forgave their errors and encouraged them to relearn how to govern from the long disuse of their talents stolen from them by their own military. Not only in the territory overtly taken from the Germans but also behind German lines we worked so, encouraging even the Partisans to civil preparation as well as to military perpetration and embodying them, as soon as victory came, into an Italian civil government in territories where the guns had barely ceased to smoke. Moreover, we opened schools under shellfire to begin teaching the Italian young that the military had no vested rights over their growing souls.

This story in Italy, where we were first getting our governmental legs, has been repeated in both Germany and Japan, with varying tempo but with no variance of determination to supplant the military by the civil authority. In Germany teams of civil experts in military uniform went in with the military not only to take over the government but to begin, from plans previously drawn, to institute electoral processes before the Germans had well recovered from their daze. We pushed elections on them not only that we might get responsible civilians but that civilians might relearn civic responsibility after their long dark night of subordination of their own accursed military. Even well before the first year of occupation was over—while other zones were but getting ready to begin to commence the evolution to which all alike were

committed at Potsdam—American forces were standing by as
helpfully as possible and with a minimum of presumption to
bring to birth constitutions in each American *Land*, constitutions that would symbolize popular sovereignty and would
implement the primacy of the German civil over even the
American military. This policy we not only broached in advance of the invasion of Germany but it we have pushed in
season and out of season, with a pertinacity matched only by
patience in overlooking the fumbling through which Germans
approach their democratic rendezvous with destiny.

What we did in Italy and Germany in this regard, we have
overmatched in Japan, if such superiority be possible. Before
the Sumari swords cooled in their scabbards, General Mac-
Arthur had prompted the Japanese to draft a constitution that
out-democratized our own (as touching the prerogatives of
the military and the radical renunciation of war); and before
the children had broken the habit of bowing to where the
portrait of the emperor no longer was, an American education
mission was called for and furnished to democratize the
schools and to begin with a shove the long push for a Japan
horizontalwise rather than overfeudalized with a military
hierarchy.

Moreover, in all these lands during this impatient process
of subordinating our military to their civil authorities, we
were busy too in transforming our own occupation into a
civilian organization with only enough of the military left
unconcealed to discourage any revival of the militaristic spirit
which had long been indigenous in all these three lands. When
the question was raised in Italy (even before the country was
half cleansed of the Germans) as to what departments of military government might with impunity be civilianized, I vol-
unteered at once to have my own, the Educational Subcom-
mission, demilitarized at the earliest possible moment, adding
that all we were doing as military men we could as well do

in civilian garb and do with better grace. The response was the same in Germany, when the question was raised in connection with Education and Religious Affairs; and in Japan the attitude has re-enacted that pattern. It is the American way and dramatizes the strength of the Constitution in our habits: a will to exchange authority for influence upon the slightest opportunity. What I have said of educational leaders in military government can be said, *pari passu*, of every branch of military government, leaving apart such functions as public safety, which is rightly the last, and that justly late, to shed the insignia of command.

Summarizing, then, our military government in the three great conquered lands as touching our first constitutional criterion—dominance of the military by the civil—we may conclude with pride that (1) we have used the necessitated priority of our military to dissolve its primacy; (2) we have in this crucial regard outdistanced all other powers with whom we have been in competition; (3) we have risked always the error of being premature rather than indulge lethargy in our commitment to civil authority over military; and (4) we have vindicated our Constitution by perpetrating it in difficult practice rather than by merely indulging the pseudo-rectitude of preaching its prime virtue.

What we conclude on this score under circumstances the most difficult—i.e., in the government of *conquered* peoples—applies with fuller force to circumstances that are ideologically easier—i.e., our government of Dependent Areas. Here the barest suggestion of our success will suffice. Italy has been an ambiguous case as to this classification. There is a historic case, however, not in the least ambiguous. It will make our point eloquently. The Philippines, got not only as a result of our defeat of Spain but also through subsequent force of arms against the Filipinos themselves, have now under our tutelage worked their way from dependence to complete freedom of our civil, as early they achieved their freedom from our military. For a nation whose military mission is to substitute by even military means a future civil for a past military order, the emancipation of the Philippines was a day of pride. Nothing could have been more appropriate than that their full independence came July 4, the first Fourth following V-J Day. It was the American spirit back of the American practice when General MacArthur remarked to General Carlos P. Romulo at the landing on Leyte: "Congress gave political equality to the Filipinos but no law could have given you social equality. You won that, on Bataan."

More subtle, if not also more tendentious for freedom than the superiority of the civil, is our constitutional separation of the secular and the sacerdotal. More subtle, it is also more difficult to achieve and to maintain. Only in America for the first hundred years of modern democracy was the logic of this separation clearly seen and courageously maintained. Russia has now joined the ranks, going America one better by separating church and school as well as church and state. Japan is now joining the ranks of the truly radical in this constitutional respect.

And such separation will remain radical when all else has become conservative, for it constitutes a "going to the very roots" of what spells conservation of the spiritual forces of mankind. It was the merest good luck, accompanied by something almost whimsically providential, that America achieved this prudent formula and wrote deeply into her Constitution this radical doctrine. All the saints groaned to high heaven at being made free from the imminent persecution of any one of their sectarianisms that might capture the state, as the Puritans had captured it in Massachusetts. Each was, of course, betting on its own success at the capture, success with the aid of the Almighty. Jefferson found the implementation of his notion of religious freedom more difficult than the abolition of primogeniture, the disestablishment of entail, and more difficult even than the early stages of popular education. The saints not only fought the separation, they spat upon him who promoted it. None was pious enough to trust his own piety without the backing of power. Each sectary regarded the world as his divine oyster and was determined, under God, to eat it—and to bite any other sectary who tried to nibble in. Truth to tell, had not there been a good many others of the Founding Fathers, like Jefferson, heterodox to the then (and yet) prevailing veneer of holiness, the world would have long lacked and might never have gained the intriguing peace that comes from the happy pluralizing of the power drive that gnaws at the vitals of all sectarian piety.

In that sad event we should now be seeing Americans as military governors foisting their religious patterns upon the conquered as briskly as would triumphant Catholics or conquering Communists. To the contrary of all this, it is the depth of American conviction in the beneficence of a social distance between power and perfection that prevents our ruthless prying of church and state apart when we find them, as we found them in Italy, locked in carnal fraternization. And yet we must admit that there are Americans *and* Americans in this respect. Roman Catholic Americans have never in general approved our constitutional doctrine separating church and state, even when they have understood it. Al Smith professed to understand it and even to approve it; but the Jesuit weekly of Smith's political heyday set him right and publicly warned the American people that Smith did not represent the church in his radical tolerance. In a communion where acceptance of sacerdotal variety is no virtue save as means to such political strength as can then subvert tolerance as a religious end, the aspiration follows the undertow: from ideological uniformity through organizational strength to sectarian domination of culture. And there are Protestants who hanker for religious public schools, forerunners though such schools would be to sectarianism's running wild once more in the preserves of power. Such sectaries apart, our Fathers, wise from experience, wrote at the portal of our sacred Bill of Rights that even "Congress shall pass no law" which would bridge, negatively or positively, this gulf dug deep between church and state. And there are Americans, thank God an adequate number as yet, who agree with the Founding Fathers sufficiently to keep tolerance firm in America, so firm that our military government has insisted upon letting religious establishments alone as they were, even when they illustrated, as in Italy, a relation with power which we ourselves deprecate and which our Constitution forbids. In Italy we permitted the alliance which the papacy had made with fascism to stand, and in Germany we have tentatively stood by the existing concordats.

For the moment passing by Japan, which might seem our exception to prove the foregoing rule, let us but briefly say what this, our constitutional separation of church and state, seems to mean. Such separation has as its chief increment, more unearned than earned, a tolerance of one religion by another or of one sect by another inside the same religion. This matter of tolerance, conceived generally, is a *sine qua non* of democracy; for without it rule by the majority is impossible or, being possible, becomes undesirably autocratic. But the tolerance must work both ways, and this is often forgotten. It works downward from the majority so that each minority may be allowed outgoing efforts, itself to become a majority. It works upward from the minority so that, while it is a minority, it will not sabotage existing legitimacy but will abide its own weakness until it can through reason and persuasion turn that weakness into electoral strength. It is this feeling for "the rules of the game" which also gives the doctrine a mien of mutuality as touching both state and church. It is always remembered that the doctrine protects the church, protects it against the tyrannical downthrust of the politically powerful, but it is often forgotten—though it is of equal importance—that it protects the state against the fanatical upthrust of sectarian meanness. It prescribes magnanimity to each as the price of its continuing freedom.

Let me return now to Japan, which seems the exception to our letting religion alone as military governors. Whether the distinction in treatment between religion in Japan and in Europe can be maintained on grounds of justice we shall consider after we have briefly described what our practice has been.

In Europe, which shares our Christian prejudice, the practice has been to disturb general religious arrangements as little as possible, consistent with the principle of letting no respectable sect be persecuted. In all of Italy and in parts of Germany (Baden, Bavaria, and Prussia) the Allies found concordats in force with the Vatican which, as interpreted, tied our hands to the status quo, as a minimum. It is advised to say "minimum"; for the Catholic church, and in Germany the Lutheran as well, with that noble impartiality of self-preference which nobody more innocently than the saints dignify, was not averse, starting with what it had, to getting all it could in a time of social unsettlement. None of the trouble we had with the church in Italy arose from our trying to avoid our minimum commitment to the concordat but rather from the church's grasping for all it could get of power. Hardly had we entered Sicily until church authorities—possibly because the military did not know either their own rights under international law or the presumption of the church as superior to human law—wrested the right to open denominational schools, which the concordat had not allowed them. Once dug in, they screamed high injustice every time the belated state schools began to claim the jurisdiction as touching standards which rightly belonged to them. There were weaklings or sentimentalists or sectarians who gave way to this grasping spirit; and our A.M.G. educational unit, before I became chief of it, went so far as to recall a pamphlet containing up-to-date hints to teachers when and because the church, which had originally passed it without complaint, recalled that an Italian scholar who, though Catholic, was anticlerical had written it. Such acts of amity on our part did not, however, discourage ecclesiastical authorities, especially those from America who loved to play at diplomacy in troubled Italian waters, from brazen presumption at every turn of the wheel of circumstance. Roving emissaries, ecclesiastical soldiers of fortune in Italy from America, made such mean and baseless representations to the Apostolic Delegation in Washington as to what they feared, or purported to fear, we were going to do in Italy that official cognizance was taken and a stinging rebuke was administered from the highest authority in the field to the church's effort to sow seeds of dissention between British and American officers for sordid religious advantage.

Without regard to provocation, however—and who can be more provocative than those who do not know for certain that they are not God?—our practice followed our policy without deviation. We finished the Italian educational venture as we had begun it, doing nothing to spread in Italy the cardinal constitutional doctrine of America, the separation of church and state. Up to whatever point prudence can be made to stretch, our American attitude toward religion permits and even at times requires us to tolerate religious intolerance. Somebody should be Christian even though the saints find the high ideal too hard.

We had neither the chance nor, practically speaking, the excuse to do in Italy what later we did in Germany of a constitutional sort. In Italy the population is so all but unanimously of one sect that religious freedom for other sects is a question which to raise (and it has been raised right along by other Christian sects) is to seem to involve soldiers in making much ado about almost nothing in the heavy backwash of war. In Germany, where the situation is different, where, indeed, religious power is happily pluralized, tolerance is more necessary to be acknowledged by law and to be dignified by constitution. We have, therefore, in Germany presumed much further than in Italy, as military governors, to articulate our constitutional principle of religious freedom: not complete separation of church and state, but a ramshackle halfway house in which for the time all sects can dwell in tentative freedom. Mid-course of constitution-making in Germany, we may note here the comments made by our Religious Affairs Branch of Military Government upon drafts of constitutions submitted for approval from the three *Länder* of the American Zone. On the draft from *Land* Württemberg-Baden (1) it was objected that constitutionally the state should not "recognize the churches and the religious and Weltanschauung societies" (as the draft phrased it) because these had a right to exist without any official cognizance whatsoever from the state and (2) it was prescribed that a clause be inserted into the constitution stating specifically that "there will be no state church." On the first draft of the constitution from Bavaria (1) it was objected that anybody should under any conditions "be obliged to disclose his religious denomination" and (2) it was prescribed that there be eliminated any doctrine of approval or even of "acknowledgment" by the state of the presence of religious communions. On the draft from Greater Hesse (1) it was objected that the state should not try in any sense "to define or to delimit the functions of the church" and (2) it was prescribed, as in the case of Württemberg-Baden, that a specific clause be inserted in the constitution against a "state church."

In Japan the treatment of religion, from our constitutional

point of view, has involved a greater distinction, it would seem, than the ideological differences between Japan and our two European enemies could justify, save by means of the sectarian justification that Europe is "Christian" and so had somebody at Washington to speak for her status quo, whereas Japan is "Pagan" and had no such voice in America. The distinction between the two seemed to me so unfair that I was instrumental in getting removed from the report of the United States Education Mission to Japan any reference whatsoever to the Christian religion (because under the circumstances any such reference would become sectarian and invidious). Since America herself is not constitutionally Christian, Japan offers us a splendid temptation to return to our constitutional *noblesse oblige*, utter neutrality as between all contending sects. In Japan, therefore, we have reinstated America's constitutional circumspection and have separated church and state.

This re-enactment has proceeded in two stages. First, General MacArthur as head of military government in Japan required the emperor to divest himself of divinity in order that he might, taking upon himself "the form of a man," be in all points tempted as his subjects were and be at length resurrected into democratic glory from this, the grave of his sovereign renunciation. Second, the constitution drafted under the auspices of our military government contained, and now the Japanese Diet has sustained, a specific separation of these two ancient incompatibilities.

The identification in Japan of the formally religious with the actual political made this separation easy without jolting our sensitivity against intervention in this intimate field of conscience. But whatever the complete accounting of our differential action in the East, Japan becomes thus the beneficiary of our constitutional wisdom as no other conquered or liberated country has become. This is another reason, of the subtlest and deepest sort, why we may well expect during the next half-century more from Japan for the fame of our American way of life in the world than from all the other conquered countries combined.

It is no mean advantage in the competition for international place when a modern state can divest itself of sectarian trammels, with all the camouflaged meanness of spirit and all its unconscious undertows against know-hows—know-hows of population control, for instance, of scientific inventiveness in general, of unprejudiced access to learning and to trade—and can achieve that largeness of spirit which religious sectarianism seems always to doom to death when it has power.

To summarize our progress in recommending to conquered peoples the second sacred canon in our constitutional trinity: In Italy we have been stopped through churchly pressure on Washington. In Germany we have been restrained by ambiguous but jealous division of power between Lutheran and Catholic sectarianism. In Japan alone have we been able to share with a foe what many feel to be our chief source of unity and strength in the continuing maelstrom of ideological fecundity, a source which complete religious freedom alone seems able to yield.

The elevation in America of the judiciary above the executive and even above the legislative is the least imperative of our three constitutional criteria, though it reflects, partly for lack of urgency but in brilliant fashion, the spirit of our whole constitutional system. It was not in point of historic fact made into, but rather it grew to be, a constitutional principle.

We have not, to come at once to the specific point, insisted upon this principle in any of our conquered territories, or even in any territory dependent upon us. Military government, as we have indicated, is a complete denial of this principle, since such government makes a totality of political power and puts into the hands not merely of one department but actually of one man all the functions of government. Since, however, it has proved the genius of our military government to abolish itself as soon as possible in deference to the first of our trinity, supremacy of the civil over the military, we may look hopefully meantime for evidences that, while consciously withering away, military government pays passing deference to this third constitutional canon, i.e., judicial supremacy.

As indicated, we have not written the principle into any of the constitutions which we have supervised. It might prove embarrassing to do so, since the doctrine is not written into our own Constitution. It might be even more embarrassing for the reason that the hegemony of any among departments of government, all of which are equal by assumption, is never granted; it is only sometimes achieved. If, however, we think of judicial pre-eminence as being the elevation of the "Word over All," including influence over power, then we shall look to our emphasis upon and to our philosophy of education in military government for the indirect deference we have paid to this principle in our postmilitary endeavors. To trust to "influence" rather than to "power" is to be on the highroad whose goal is the citadel of legal adjudication of all human disputes. Education is the institutional method of implementing our trust in "influence."

Not only we have had an educational division in all our military governments (early and successful efforts were made to recruit and to train educational specialists on the same basis as other governmental specializations), but we have assigned these educators honorable place for the fulfilment of their important functions. In Italy the function of education was made of cabinet rank, so to say; in Germany it has been a "Branch" along with (for historic reasons) Religious Affairs, but having an honorable place, with its advice trusted and for the most part followed by the commander-in-chief. In Japan it has also been a "Branch" rather than a Division. But more important than differential rank and place is the fact that educators have been everywhere present to direct educational efforts and have been backed up as much as other specialists in military government.

So much for the emphasis upon education in military government. Under that emphasis the philosophy of education which has been directed and pursued is equally important in dramatizing our trust in that branch of civil government which puts its faith in processes of reason for the overdirection of human affairs. If we had gone forth armed with educational dogma to convert conquered peoples to "progressive" education or to "scholastic" education or to anything less universal than just education, we should have under the guise of reason been resorting to pressure that goes with legislation or the focused energy that inspires executive action. This we have not done, not in any land; but we have more nearly approached it in Japan than elsewhere.

In Italy I investigated as a matter of principle and defended against all activists, however "progressive," a policy of negativity: Never tell the Italians what to do but only what not to do. As put in my final report to the Allied Commission:

Our mission in Italy was negative: we came to destroy fascism, not this time officially to make the world safe for democracy. . . . My thought has steadily been: that war permits little that is positive to be done in the delicate field of education but puts full temptation before educators to act so as to make the positive permanently impossible; that to resist the temptation to play at power is to play for time to reorient Italy after the war; and that, other conditions favoring, we may presently (exchanging books, students, teachers, and certainly ideals) come among Italian scholars to take the place of affection long held by Germany. . . . Most of all, and all the while, we have done whatever we have done through methods of consultation and in an atmosphere of democratic reasonableness, to make right procedures speak where commands of authority would not carry beyond the echo of the hour.

In Germany, Colonel John W. Taylor and Colonel Marshall Knappen have pursued their own versions of the same philosophic emphasis, for the same general reasons. Colonel Knappen, operating in the religious field, was subject to the American tradition of noninterventionism, applied to protect even the bad provided that it be not too bad. Colonel Taylor has outwritten his education policy with suggestions as to reasons, so that he who runs may read: "It is the policy of the Education Branch," says he, "to leave the Germans whatever does not conflict with the program of denazification and demilitarization of Germany. In the field of education no textbook has been forced upon the Germans. It is believed that self-determination along democratic lines guarantees better results in the end."

In that declaration is reflected from the military-government field, and in circumstances that can be more tempting to intervention than a mere observer might think, the faith in reason and the patience with gradualism which together raised to supremacy the American judiciary, a department of government which can only speak, unable to vote itself a single dollar to live on or a solitary policeman to hide behind.

It is the selfsame American faith which in Japan has kept education circumspect in a field of force—circumspect, but not so covered as in Italy or so passive as in Germany. The differential in Japan has been in largest part the Japanese people themselves. The United States Education Mission to Japan, intent upon observing cultural amenities within the general field of noninterventionism, came away only after having intervened to a remarkable degree in remaking Japanese education. But the Japanese would not have it otherwise. For whatever reason, they wish to be democratized; and so the report of this mission reflects a differential policy in Japan. So runs the report:

It has been brought home to us by the Japanese educators themselves that even the wisest negations are not enough: they demand and require of us some positive guidance. They state freely that they know the words "liberalism, democracy, science, and humanism" but that they do not always sense the fundamental meaning and may be unable to chart the painful road toward implementation.

The intent to rely in education upon reasonableness has, however, in all the lands been the same; only the degree of intervention has been different. The difference does not oppose in spirit the judicial principle that men and cultures shall be self-determinative, save only as they forfeit the right or renounce the desire to be so. The Japanese forfeited their right to pursue their own aggressive positivity, but they have renounced the desire to be let alone in their struggle toward democracy.

So much for educational policy in military government, which I have chosen strategically in order to evaluate our devotion in conquered countries to our constitutional doctrine of judicial supremacy and through which I have sought to illustrate finally our whole constitutional trinity. It is not as though we had not had our courts all the while functioning in conquered territories. It is in part that military courts are not so good an example of the trust in reason as is education, under military government. Military courts are, of course, subject finally to the will of the commanding officer and so are not so immune to caprice as civil courts ought to be. It is in part also that the philosophy whereby courts function is not so evident through the courts as it is through the educational process. Courts seek to do the reasonable thing to people who have themselves done the unreasonable thing. Education seeks to promote the course of reason before life itself has been warped by unreasonable action.

And yet it would not be circumspect to close this section without a word upon that conspicuous judicial assize just closed at Nuremberg, Germany. It is a conspicuous, if not quite unsullied, symbol of the finality which we ascribe to reason even in military government. I say not quite "unsullied" not to carp but merely to observe the deviation of a justice that is dealt out by conquerors along lines completely effective ex post facto. But the other side of Nuremberg—and it is more important—is that instead of summarily shooting men who by their own preaching and practice had forfeited the right to live, we have hanged them only after a trial, an open trial, with counsel and witnesses and a hearing patient beyond past precedent. We have given abominable villains a trial which some of them have had the lingering decency to admit was "fair." This is testified to also by the fruits: not all were punished alike; not all, indeed, were grievously punished; not all were even punished. Those who were executed went to their deaths under the symbol of justice and with the bittersweet music of retributive rationality ringing in their ears.

Those who went, had to go (either summarily or judicially), for their offense was final: they refused to play the game of collective life according to the rules of reason. Not only did they flout all preceding rules. They represented, in all conquered lands, the lack of patience to elaborate new rules. It was the essence of the dynamism which to both fascism and naziism glorified the "New Order" that the life of the strong knows no rational rules; that, indeed, the rules of the game may be changed by the strong at any and every stage of the game. Such men do not belong to any team—and the good of the game requires that they go.

They are gone—or going.

It is the final glory of our military government—and I like to include in "our" the British, with whom we fully shared responsibility in Italy, with whom we jointly planned occupation policies for Germany, and from whose long colonial experience we have profited in Japan—that it played the game according to the best rules of the past and is now prepared to improve the rules for the future, in the light of the horrors of war and of our self-disclosed deficiencies.

It is that sense of the game and that respect for its rules that the game may go on, which characterizes Anglo-American jurisprudence, which informs our American constitutional trinity. Our military government the world over has reflected, under circumstances adverse to reason, the spirit in which civilized life has been formed, the spirit of a game played by rules which themselves evolve as the game goes forward from season to season.

In spite of many failures under the hard hand of practice, this was the spirit of our enterprise up to the very top and unto the latest hour. General Eisenhower, the supreme commander-in-chief, grasped the extended hand of Field Marshal Montgomery and concluded the longest, the bitterest, and the most portentous controversy of the war—concluded it as friends—when he wrote: "In whatever years are left to both of us, possibly we may occasionally meet, not only to reminisce, but to exemplify the spirit of comradeship that I trust will exist between our two countries for all time."

This spirit was kept alive by the joint sharing of the imagery with which Montgomery summarized both the tensions between them and the final release:

When Allies work together there are bound to be different points of view, and when these occur it is essential that they are thrashed out fully and frankly; but once a final decision is given, it is the duty of all members of the team to carry out that decision loyally. The Allied team worked in this spirit, and by its teamwork achieved overwhelming victory.

THE MILITARY AND FOREIGN POLICY

QUINCY WRIGHT

✷

"THE problem of civil-military relationships," writes Charles E. Merriam, "is not solely one of the democracies, but a continuing problem of all political associations—a problem of the reconciliation of policy and strategy, of statesman and soldier." When the military has been overemphasized in this relationship, government has been called "militaristic"; and when it has been underemphasized, government has been called "weak." A balance seems to have been considered desirable.

I propose to consider some of the dangers that arise from an over- or underemphasis upon the military in foreign policy and then to consider the extent to which the organization and practice of the United States have avoided these dangers.

The military may be thought of as an instrument of government or as an influence on government. It consists, on the one hand, of an organization of men, materials, and ideas ready to enforce the law or policy established by the government and, on the other hand, of the complex of attitudes and opinions of the members of that organization ready to influence the government's decisions on law or policy. Either the military machine or the military mind may be exaggerated and also either of them may be depreciated.

The military mind has been criticized in many quarters. Pacifists usually find it barbarous and inhuman, and statesmen sometimes find it narrow and unadaptable. Clemenceau remarked that war is too serious a business to intrust to the

military. Specifically, it has been charged with lack of inventiveness, traditionalism, and an incapacity to perceive
when weapons or methods have become obsolete. H. A.
DeWeerd writes:

The civilian mind was somewhat quicker to see the war [World
War I] as an intensified clash between old forms and new forces than
was the military. To the latter the titanic clash between the Allied
and Central Powers was like any other war—except that it was
bigger. They were prepared to wage war in just one way—the field
service regulations way. With what must be described as instinct,
they distrusted the introduction of new elements in the struggle. The
history of the misuse of gas by the German High Command and of
the tanks by the British High Command offer illustrations in point.
Both of these weapons were forced on the military by civilian pressure. But when they were employed it was done so timidly and so
experimentally, with such a limited view of the potentialities of
both weapons, that the surprise factor was wasted for trivial local
gains. . . . Professional soldiers could not invent; invention had been
properly drilled out of them. Pride and traditional reserve restrained
them in some cases from using the devices of "outsiders."

Perhaps a more balanced judgment is given by Bernard
Brodie, who has devoted unusual attention to relations between the naval mind and naval invention:

Men who have been condemned out of hand as unimaginative or
unprogressive may simply have been much more acutely aware of
technical difficulties to be overcome before a certain invention could
be useful than were their more optimistic contemporaries. The mere
circumstance that one man was proved wrong in his predictions and
another right does not prove that the latter was the more discerning
observer.

The military mind has also been charged with an irrational
conviction of the inevitability of war. Military writers, such
as Clausewitz, Bernhardi, and Mahan, have certainly been
skeptical about plans for world organization and universal
peace. "Peace," said General von Moltke, "is a dream and not

even a beautiful dream." There are, of course, exceptions, but it is perhaps to be expected that military men would not easily contemplate the termination of their profession.

Another charge against the military mind is overconfidence in the military method as applicable to the solution of all problems. Clashes between foreign offices and military offices have occurred in all governments. During the American Civil War, Secretary of the Navy Gideon Welles, advised by his admirals, was continually urging more vigorous enforcement of the blockade by seizure of neutral vessels irrespective of protest which might come from Britain and other states. He was thus often in controversy with Secretary of State Seward, who felt that avoidance of serious friction with the great European states was essential. More recently, the Navy's pressure for island bases in the Pacific and elsewhere has clashed with the State Department's interest in avoiding an appearance of imperialistic land-grabbing contrary to the principles of the Atlantic Charter, the Cairo Declaration, and the Charter of the United Nations. The history of World War I shows how frequently Tirpitz and Ludendorff insisted on policies which added to the number of Germany's enemies. Hitler and Mussolini likewise gave great weight to military considerations.

The military mind with rare exceptions has favored military preparedness in time of peace. In America, Washington's advice, "The only way to obtain peace is to be prepared for war," is part of the military vocabulary. Military and naval men have habitually urged an increase in the military budget and an increase in military personnel. They have seldom opposed peacetime conscription.

The military mind has also tended, at least in modern times, to be patriotic and nationalistic. Attitude measurements indicate that favorableness to war and patriotism generally go together. This is not surprising since the prime objective of military activity is preservation of the national integrity, prestige, and power. A profession is likely to regard its objective as of major importance.

Finally, the military mind has tended to favor discipline, order, planning, and even regimentation in economic and social as well as military life. There has, however, been considerable variation among the military of different countries. In America military men have often recognized the value of encouraging free enterprise for military production. In Germany, on the other hand, the military have generally favored regimented government extending to all fields of life. The Hohenzollerns initiated this system and the Nazis carried it to extremes. Albert Speer, the Nazi minister of armaments production, stated that "we were at a great disadvantage because our rearmament had been planned too long on a theoretic basis." As a civilian he deplored the extent to which totalitarian planning and regimentation under military impetus had sought to organize national economy, and he tried to modify this condition, with some success. It is not surprising that the leaders of a military organization, which necessarily operates by orders from the top down, should prefer an administered plan to free competition as the basis of economic production and social order

I recently heard a military man publicly recommend that opinion in the United States should be educated to believe that war is inevitable and that when war comes the United States will have no friends, will be attacked without warning, and will be at a disadvantage if the government is hampered by democratic procedures and has failed to organize industry for military purposes. That, I think, illustrates the military mind at work.

These charges against the military mind illustrate the distortion which is characteristic of the outlook of all professional men—physicians, teachers, lawyers, or clergymen—no less than soldiers and sailors. Intensive training and practice in any field tends to beget satisfaction with its traditional methods, conviction that the conditions which constitute its *raison d'être* will persist, interest in maintaining its professional standards, conviction of the importance of its goals, and a tendency to extend its methods into other fields. The member of a profession can hardly fail to realize, though sometimes the realization may be subconscious, that augmentation of the general importance of his profession in the estimation of society will augment his own opportunities for advancement within it. Furthermore, because of his study of his profession, he has a superior capacity to state the benefits which society derives from it. Finally, because his professional activity compels him continually to look at problems from one point of view, he is likely to become incapacitated properly to weigh factors readily observed from another point of view. A professional man's interest, knowledge, and point of view conspire to distort his judgment. Professional military men are perhaps no more affected by this distortion than other professional men, but that many of them suffer from it cannot be doubted.

It is easier for the civilian than for the military man to see that efficient preparation for the use of military force as an instrument of policy tends to increase the willingness of the government to utilize that method; tends to arouse apprehension in other governments; and tends to induce them to increase their military preparations, thus precipitating an armaments race from which war is likely to eventuate. The very efficiency of preparedness tends to convert the nation from a defensive to an aggressive policy; to convert other nations from friends or allies to rivals or enemies; and to prevent any relative gain in armaments over those of rivals, with the consequence of making the sense of security less, both for the state which initiates preparedness and for all others.

These consequences of military preparation are not inevitable. The constitutions, traditions, and cultures of states differ. Some do not easily become aggressive, even with powerful armaments; some arouse less anxiety in neighbors by preparedness than do others; and some are less disturbed than others by their neighbors' preparations. Furthermore, the relation between the rate of armament building and the general political situation is of profound importance in determining psychological and political reactions. Too little military preparation may be as dangerous to the equilibrium of power as too much.

The civilian, viewing national military policy as only one element in a complex of national politics and world politics continually affected by technological, economic, and social changes, is less likely than the military man to be led away by oversimplified arguments. It may be true that an adequate military machine provides insurance against aggression, security to the national economy, and weight to the national foreign policy; but "adequacy" may fail from too rapid as well as from too slow development. Civilians who have graduated from the horse-and-buggy to the air age will not accept the common military assumption that the adequacy of the military machine is to be judged by its magnitude or by its quality in terms of past experience in the use of the military method. If experience in communicating by pony express helps little in communicating by radio, why should the experience in fighting with armored knights, with rifle brigades, or with battleships help much in fighting with air-borne atom bombs? May not technical progress affect strategy as well as tactics? May it not even affect the basic assumptions of military policy?

Aware of the characteristics of the military mind, civilians, when their voices have been of importance, have usually insisted upon the subordination of the military to the civilian authorities in policy-making. They are impressed by the greater insight even in military policy frequently shown by civilians. Lloyd George in England and Rathenau in Germany seemed to have appreciated better than the military men the character of World War I as a production enterprise and the importance of bringing the national economy into full utilization for war purposes.

The civilian has had more confidence than the military man in the possibility of politically organizing the world for peace. He has not regarded war as inevitable in particular places and during particular periods of time.

The civilian has also realized that military preparedness is but one element in national security. The country best prepared at the outbreak of a war has commonly won the first battles but lost the war. The militarily prepared government tends to be aggressive or to be suspected by others of having aggressive intentions. Less-prepared states have, therefore, tended to ally themselves against it; and when war develops, in spite of initial losses, they have usually prevailed. In modern history national industry, national morale, national science, and international friendship seem to have made greater contributions to winning wars than the military machines available at their outset. Furthermore, the development of these instruments of security has had little tendency to stimulate the initiation of war. If excessive military preparedness is of doubtful value in maintaining national security, it is of even more dubious value in promoting national prosperity. Though military and naval authorities have widely advertised the virtue of preparedness as insurance to the national economy, history suggests that, if exaggerated, its value for this purpose is negative, both because it is costly and because it encourages unsuccessful wars.

While civilians have been alert to the exaggeration of the military mind, that mind has often been equipped with information and experience which can ill be lost to national councils. Winston Churchill regretted the failure of the admirals to volunteer their opinions when the Dardanelles expedition was being considered in 1915; and Major General Upton presents convincing evidence of the unnecessary losses endured by the United States in its wars because the advice of the professionals was ignored. The problem is clearly not one of dispensing with professional military advice or of neglecting military preparedness but of weighing this advice with many other considerations which may be overlooked by the military machine and of keeping preparedness within reason.

Confidence in the military machine as an instrument of policy is not confined to military men. Autocratic rulers have equipped themselves with praetorian guards to crush domestic revolts and have built armies to engaged in external conquest. Constitutional governments have occasionally utilized military methods for conquest, but they have sought to prevent their use for domestic oppression. British constitutional development, particularly during the seventeenth century, centered about parliamentary efforts to prevent the monarchs from establishing a military force which might be used for the suppression of popular liberties. People have wanted the state's armed forces to be efficient for defense against external aggression but inefficient for domestic tyranny and have found it difficult to achieve both objectives. Various forms of military force—militia, conscript armies, mercenaries, long-service professionals, and volunteer armies—and various forms of control—executive, legislative, local, and divided—have been proposed as means to solve this problem. The problem has been less difficult when defense could be naval, for navies have proved of little use for domestic oppression.

Herbert Spencer distinguished the military society, which relies on the armed forces for domestic order and foreign security, from the industrial society, which relies on rising standards of living to assure domestic satisfaction and international co-operation to assure security. He recognized, however, that for the latter purpose no state has been able entirely to dispense with armed force. Some capacity for defense has been a necessary condition of diplomacy in maintaining peaceful international relations among sovereign states.

While the military way cannot meet all problems, it has been indispensable for some; and the danger of inadequate military organization for states that wish to survive has often been indicated by history. Upton noted the following causes of military weakness of the United States in 1881 when he wrote his treatise published by the government in 1904 under the title *The Military Policy of the United States:*

1. The employment of militia and undisciplined troops commanded by generals and officers utterly ignorant of the military art.

2. Short enlistments from three months to three years, instead of for or during the war.

3. Reliance upon voluntary enlistments, instead of voluntary enlistments coupled with conscription.

4. The intrusion of the States in military affairs and the consequent waging of all our wars on the theory that we are a confederacy instead of a nation.

5. Confusing volunteers with militia and surrendering to the States the right to commission officers of volunteers the same as officers of militia.

6. The bounty—a national consequence of voluntary enlistments.

7. The failure to appreciate military education, and to distribute trained officers as batallion, regimental and higher commanders in our volunteer armies.

8. The want of territorial recruitment and regimental depots.

9. The want of post-graduate schools to educate our officers in strategy and the higher principles of the art of war.

10. The assumption of command by the Secretary of War.

Upton emphasized particularly the inadequacy of the state-controlled militia system. The makers of the Constitution intended the state militias, when called into national service as provided by Congress, to serve as the main reliance for internal order and external defense. The failure of Massachusetts and Connecticut to co-operate in a federal call for the militia during the War of 1812 brought the following remarks from President Madison:

The refusal was founded on a novel and unfortunate exposition of the provisions of the Constitution relating to the militia. . . . It is obvious that if the authority of the United States to call into service and command the militia for the public defense can be thus frustrated even in a state of declared war, and, of course, under apprehensions of invasion preceding war, they are not one nation for the purpose most of all requiring it.

The United States has now through a process of constitutional construction and legislative enactment developed a military system independent of state-controlled militias, but the situation faced by Madison is worthy of recollection because the military force relied upon by the United Nations is even more divided among sovereign nations. If American experience is considered, it appears probable that the United Nations will be obliged to organize a unified force, independent of the control of particular nations if it is to carry out its objectives in maintaining international peace and security. It was reported on October 12, 1946, that certain members of the Military Staff Committee of the United Nations, which had been laboring on the problem of organizing a United Nations military policy for six months, had come to the conclusion that "abolition of national military forces and the establishment of a single international force under the United Nations was the only sure path of continuing peace."

The military machine must be sufficiently large and sufficiently centralized to prevent successful challenge to the community's constitution by any of its parts. But such a machine can be used for oppression. The solution is to be found in civilian constitutional control. This is no less true in the world community now necessary than it has been in the national communities which have, during the past few centuries, set the limits of reliable law and order.

How has the United States Constitution dealt with the problems of military influence on policy and of control of the military machine?

Through most of its history the military mind has probably had too little rather than too much influence in the United States; and the military machine has probably generally been too small rather than too large.

Military officers have been elected to the presidency, but it cannot be said that such men as Washington, Jackson, William Henry Harrison, Taylor, Grant, Hayes, Benjamin Harrison, McKinley, and Theodore Roosevelt displayed many characteristics of the military mind while occupying that position. Military officers in service have at times exercised considerable influence on policy during wars. Naval officers, even in times of peace, made policies in the early relations with the Barbary States and the far eastern states. The Army immediately after the Civil War and the Navy in Theodore Roosevelt's time attained magnitudes which made it possible for the president to employ them as "big sticks" in diplomacy. In the main, however, American foreign policy has been made by civilians, and the armed forces have been small in proportion to the size of the nation. There has been considerable justification for the complaint of Major General Upton, written in 1881:

Our military policy, or, as many would affirm, our want of it, has now been tested during more than a century. It has been tried in foreign, domestic and Indian wars, and while military men, from painful experience, are united as to its defects and dangers, our final success in each conflict has so blinded the popular mind, as to induce the belief that as a nation we are invincible. . . .

Whether we may be willing to admit it or not, in the conduct of war, we have rejected the practice of European nations and with little variation, have thus far pursued the policy of China.

All of our wars have been prolonged for want of judicious and economical preparation, and often when the people have impatiently awaited the tidings of victory those of humiliating defeat have plunged the nation into mourning.

The cause of all this is obvious to the soldier and should be no less obvious to the statesman. It lies partly in the unfounded jealousy of not a large, but even a small standing army; in the persistent use of raw troops; in the want of an expansive organization, adequate for every prospective emergency; in short and voluntary enlistments, carrying with them large bounties; and in a variety of other defects. . . .

In every country save our own, the inability of unprofessional men to command armies would be accepted as a self-evident proposition.

The civilian government was not, however, impressed by Upton's document, which remained in the archives until resurrected by Secretary of War Root a generation later. In the twentieth century it has had some influence.

Nonprofessionals have difficulty in shaking from the back of their minds the thought that "all's well that ends well" and that maybe there is virtue in improvising defense after emergencies have arisen. While they would admit that such improvisation has its cost, it may have the advantage of escaping the professional's reluctance to abandon obsolete methods; his hesitation to utilize the most advanced science, invention, and engineering; and his prejudice against recommendations of able nonprofessional minds. Improvisation may have the virtue of escaping the dead hand of tradition and routine; the virtue of invoking a national sense of participation and initiative in business, labor, agriculture, and society as a whole; the virtue of stimulating individual self-reliance; and the virtue of assuring that politics—the art of changing the minds of men, whether those men are nationals, allies, neutrals, or enemies—will remain the master-art, of which the use of force is only one instrument.

Secretary of State Bryan's suggestion in 1915 that prepared-ness was unnecessary, because in case of hostile attack a million men would leap from their plows like Cincinnatus, was hardly adapted to the military technique of the time. He, however, expressed in exaggerated form the skepticism of the average American about professional military advice.

Is this situation changing? Are Americans abandoning their confidence in military improvisation and their doubt of profes-sional military advice? A recent report of the Foreign Policy Association of New York asserts that "the War and Navy De-partments, and army and naval officers today participate in the formulation and execution of foreign policy to a degree unknown in any former peacetime period." In support of this proposition, attention is called to President Truman's recom-mendation on June 15, 1946, that "Congress give a permanent place to military agencies in the making of foreign policy." The Foreign Policy Report continues:

He proposed "the establishment of a Council of National Defense, in which a Secretary of National Defense (who would combine the present duties of the Secretaries of War and Navy) would have au-thority to make decisions with the Secretary of State for the integra-tion of American, foreign and military policies." Congress gave ef-fect to the proposal in the National Security Act of 1947.

Attention was also called to the policy of military exchange with Latin America, to United States military aid to China, to naval influence in the policy of acquiring bases in the Pacific, to acceptance of long-term responsibilities in the occupation of enemy territories in Europe and Asia, and to the utilization of military men such as General Marshall, Lieutenant General W. B. Smith, Major General John H. Hilldring, and Major General Frank R. McCoy in important diplomatic and State Department positions. Furthermore, military and naval appropriations have remained at a very high level, and the naval demonstration of the atom bomb at Bikini could be construed as a political demonstration. Some of these matters were referred to by Secretary of Commerce Wallace in his letter to the President on July 23, 1946. He thought they made it appear "either that we are preparing ourselves to win the war which we regard as inevitable or that we are trying to build up a predominance of force to intimidate the rest of mankind."

Other indications of a change of opinion in regard to the influence of the military upon foreign policy is to be found in the development of such agencies as the president's personal military and naval advisers, and the State, War, and Navy Co-ordinating Committee (S.W.N.C.C.). Though the latter consisted of civilian assistant secretaries of each of the three departments, under the chairmanship of the assistant secretary of state, its meetings were attended by high naval and military officers. These arrangements give the military an opportunity to exercise direct influence upon foreign policy.

Mention may also be made of the support accorded by both the American government and the American people to the emphasis in the United Nations Charter upon the organization of military power under a United Nations military staff committee of professional military men. This emphasis is in contrast to the historic American opinion that international peace was to be maintained by disarmament and arbitration. It is not surprising that the ill-success of that thesis should have encouraged reconsideration. But the results of reconsideration mark a significant change of the American attitude toward the military.

World War II, which drew into active service a larger proportion of the American population than any previous war, has left the American people with a greater disposition than at any previous time to trust professional military opinion and to employ the military method in foreign policy. It is clear that if armies increase in size and if military experience extends to a larger and larger proportion of the population, the military mind is more likely to become characteristic of the national mind.

Is this new opinion in accord with the American constitutional tradition? Is it appropriate for realization of American foreign policy objectives?

The Constitution applied the system of checks and balances to military affairs as to all others. The president is commander-in-chief of the Army and Navy. He can direct the military forces and make international agreements on military matters. He can even utilize military forces on his own responsibility to carry out international obligations, to enforce national laws, and to defend national territory, American citizens, and accepted national policies in time of peace. The president, therefore, has broad opportunities to utilize the military machine as an instrument of policy.

The powers of Congress to declare war, to authorize reprisals, and to make rules of military capture have not substantially limited the president's power to use for broad national purposes whatever military forces Congress may have made available.

The exclusive power of Congress to provide for calling-forth the militia has become unimportant because the militia as such has ceased to be important in the military machine. In this respect the intention of the Constitution has been modified through the development by Congress of national forces as a major instrument of national military policy.

The control of Congress lies not in checking or regulating the president's use of armed forces but in controlling the size of the armed forces available to him. Congress alone can make appropriations and provide for raising an army, maintaining a navy, and making rules for their government. Army appropriations cannot be for longer than two years. Congress has often provided for less military force than the president has wanted. This check may be reduced by congressional legislation or international agreements committing the United States to maintain military, naval, and air contingents of specified size for international policing purposes.

There is also a check upon military influence on foreign policy in the laws and orders which define the functions of the State and Defense departments. Foreign affairs are assigned to the former department. Furthermore, the tradition which excluded professional military men from the secretary-ships of the War and Navy departments has assured civilian influence in the activity of these departments. The National Security Act of 1947 required that the secretary of defense be appointed from civilian life. He, however, and the secretaries of army and navy (and air forces) are, of course, influenced by their professional subordinates.

The president, it is true, may be and has on several occasions been a professional military man, but it is the intention of the Congress and of tradition that he shall receive advice on foreign policy only from the civilian Department of State and advice on military policy only from the civilian heads of the Defense departments. This expectation has always been modified in time of war when the military and naval activities necessarily involve foreign policy and the president, as commander-in-chief, necessarily maintains continuing contact with military and naval officers. As already noted, military influence on foreign policy has increased in recent years and promises to continue to do so even in time of peace.

It would appear that neither the Constitution nor Congress can prevent the increase of professional military influence if the president, supported by public opinion, considers such influence expedient. The weight of the influence will, of course, be affected by the size of the military establishment and the character of military education, both of which are under the control of Congress. Obviously, under conditions of an armed world in which national security rests on capacity for self-defense, Congress is not likely to impair the efficiency of the armed services or their capacity to maintain America's position in the balance of power.

The danger to the democratic way of life of militarization of foreign policy and national opinion cannot be denied. Military organization relies on discipline and compulsion, and the line of authority flows from the top down. Democratic organization relies on individual initiative and consent, and the line of authority flows from public opinion at the grass roots up to the top. When a nation becomes an army, it ceases to be a democracy.

Furthermore, under world conditions in which foreign policy must be conducted by force and threats of force, centralization of power in the executive and subordination of domestic policy and congressional and public opinion to executive decisions is essential if that policy is to be effective. This is more true today than ever before, since in an atomic war, survival would depend on an organization of industry and a discipline of population to protect as large a proportion as possible from atomic destruction and to assure capacity to attack the enemy and destroy its power of retaliation as soon as possible. Military control of the sources of opinion and policy and military regimentation of national life have, however, in past civilizations stifled democracy, and they are more likely to do so today than ever before.

What remedy can democracy find to assure its survival? Is it faced by the dilemma of national destruction or militarization? It is believed that the only solution lies in a modification of world order so that states can rely upon law rather than upon their own forces for security. Today a world of power politics is even less safe for democracy than it was in Woodrow Wilson's time. Great democracies have in the past existed in a world of power politics because they could rely upon geographical isolation or upon an autocratic control of foreign policy even if domestic policy was democratically controlled. Small democracies have survived because they were protected by the power of great allies or by the rivalries of their great neighbors. In a world shrinking in transport and communication time, with domestic and foreign policy becoming indistinguishable, with the atom bomb threatening unparalleled destruction, and with great concentrations of national power in a few states, a balance of military power cannot be stable and states cannot rely for security on distance or peaceful intention. Power politics under such conditions is certain to be dangerous to all states, particularly to those who are not prepared to use the latest military devices promptly and efficiently.

The United Nations Charter has declared in principle a change in the world order from power politics to law, and it has set up institutions which may facilitate the change in practice through interpretation, application, supplementary agreements, and amendments to the Charter.

The United Nations does not, however, today assure security. States must still rely on their power or on that of their allies or protectors, feeble as that reliance is. The United Nations cannot effect the transition unless vigorously pressed to do so by a world public opinion prepared to place humanity above the nation and to develop the power of the United Nations so that it can be relied upon to put a dominant force behind universal law.

Force without law is tyranny. Law without force is anarchy. The world is still an anarchy, and states may feel compelled to become tyrannies. Only if force and law are joined in a world organization can humanity enjoy the privilege of peace and states the freedom to be democratic.

Pending such a development, the United States must remain strong; but it must prevent militarism from permeating its institutions, and it must labor to develop the world order to a condition of stability and legality. Foreign policy necessarily puts national security first, and under present conditions military policy is a major element in security. The United States cannot rely on geography in a shrinking world or on diplomacy in a world of power politics or on good will in a world where military power has a capacity for attack from transoceanic distances, with unparalleled speed and incredible violence.

The possibility of co-ordinating foreign policy and military policy through better presidential staffing; better presidential and State Department military intelligence from nonmilitary sources; better cabinet debate among the secretaries of state, defense, army, and navy; better administrative organization of the Defense departments to facilitate control by the civilian chiefs; and development of the National Security Council and the National Security Resources Board, established by the act of 1947, should therefore be explored. The interdepartmental board may not be an entirely satisfactory device for formulating policy because it tends to produce compromises rather than workable policies. It may, however, be a useful means for assembling information and co-ordinating the execution of policies set forth in general terms by presidential directive.

Co-ordination of military and foreign policy may also be facilitated at lower levels through informal contacts of State Department officials with officials of the Defense departments in Washington. Such contacts may also be maintained in the field in times of military occupation or of naval visit to foreign ports. I recall the regular discussions between the American consul and the officers of several American destroyers at Beyrouth during the Syrian disturbance of 1925. The United States had never accepted the superiority of the foreign office representative in such circumstances, as have other countries. Possibilities of rapid communication make such an organization of authority of agencies abroad less important than in earlier times, but it would appear that a general rule of State Department control on matters of foreign policy should be acknowledged in the field as in Washington.

Probably the recent union of the Army, the Navy, and the Air Force in a single department of national defense has been advisable, particularly because such a union puts air power on a parity with the two older branches of the armed forces. In that position the Air Force can develop with less interference its particular strategy aimed directly at the industrial heart of the enemy. It is true that division and occasional rivalry of the Army and Navy may have sometimes proved a useful check upon militarization of the government. Conflicting professional opinions have sometimes given an opportunity for civilian opinions to prevail. Such conflicts, however, valuable as they may have been to prevent militarization, may be suicidal for defense under present conditions. This was realized when the Joint Chiefs of Staff was organized to assure Army and Navy unity in conducting the war and to permit effective American military collaboration with Great Britain in the combined Chiefs of Staff. The greater military efficiency of a permanent union of the three military arms, coupled with a capacity for all three to develop their independent methods, cannot today be dispensed with.

While it is unwise to be dogmatic about future strategy, it is possible that the long-ranging air arm equipped with atom bombs will emerge as the major military instrument. The Army and Navy may become supplementary agencies for the defense of territory and bases, the policing of surrendered and backward areas, and the performance of United Nations services in preventing war among lesser countries. With such a development, however, it seems clear that war would have become too destructive to be justified by any policy. Statesmen will have to hasten its elimination by institutions giving to universal law and peaceful procedures an authority upon which they can rely. To such a policy the United States is committed.

Development of agencies for co-ordinating foreign policy in economic, social, and cultural fields might provide a valuable check to undesirable extension of military influence in these fields and at the same time strengthen the United Nations. The Department of State has in fact already organized interdepartmental agencies in each of these fields parallel to the Security Council in the field of defense. The Executive Committee on Economic Foreign Policy, the International Social Policy Committee, and the National Advisory Council on International Monetary and Financial Problems each includes the Department of State and other relevant departments in these fields. Such an arrangement of interdepartmental committees under the leadership of the Department of State may serve to gear the United States government into the work of the United Nations and its related agencies. It must be realized, however, that too much co-ordination of policy on the national level may prevent adequate co-ordination on the international level. Each specialized national agency should have considerable freedom to develop policy in its field through discussion with similar agencies of other countries. The national departments should be so organized as to contribute to building a world order based on law supported by universal opinion, without jeopardizing the military efficiency of the United States so long as that order remains unreliable.

National security without militarization, international co-operation without weakness, and a world law maintained by an efficient world organization supported by universal opinion —such are the goals which foreign policy and military policy must have in mind. With such goals of national and international policy the armed forces and the foreign service may both serve as valuable instruments, and the military and civilian minds may supplement rather than frustrate one another.

CIVIL-MILITARY RELATIONS IN THE UNITED NATIONS

ADLAI STEVENSON

✵

IN MANY respects the United Nations is a pioneer organization. While it has a foundation in the pre-war international organizations such as the League of Nations and the Permanent Court of International Justice, it departs radically from the pre-war patterns. In no part of the organization are these departures more apparent than in the arrangements laid down in the Charter for civil-military relations.

The subject is so new and the developments have been so recent and so meager in this field that any conclusions must be highly tentative. We have not yet reached a point where we can see more than the vague outlines of the type of military organization which the United Nations will succeed in setting up in accordance with the Charter.

For myself, my work with the United Nations has not been closely connected either with the Military Staff Committee, which has the technical responsibility under the Charter for the United Nations military organization, or with the Security Council, to which the Military Staff Committee reports. However, I have from a little distance observed the organization of the Military Staff Committee, its work, and its relations with the Security Council.

While I am happy to give you some personal observations and to suggest some of the problems, I must emphasize that what I have to say is wholly personal and in no sense official.

You are undoubtedly familiar with the general structure of

the United Nations. Its chief organs, as you know, are the General Assembly, the Security Council, the Economic and Social Council, the Trusteeship Council, the International Court of Justice, and the Secretariat. The Trusteeship Council has not yet been organized, and the International Court of Justice is only remotely concerned with civil-military relations.

The General Assembly, under Article 11, paragraph 2, may discuss any question relating to the maintenance of international peace and security and, except where the Security Council is itself dealing with the matter, may make recommendations to the states concerned or to the Security Council. Furthermore, the General Assembly may call the attention of the Security Council to situations which are likely to endanger international peace. However, if any direct action under the Charter is called for, the General Assembly, under Article 11 of the Charter, must refer the matter to the Security Council either before or after discussing it.

The General Assembly also is empowered to recommend measures for the peaceful adjustment of any situation, regardless of origin, which may impair the general welfare or friendly relations among nations, including situations resulting from violations of the purposes and principles of the Charter. It also may consider and make recommendations regarding the principles governing disarmament and the regulation of armaments. It is apparent that the Assembly is not excluded from considering the political-military field of international relations. At the same time its interest is in a sense residual and secondary and more of an advisory than of an executive character.

The Economic and Social Council is only remotely interested in the military aspects of the United Nations activities, although it has authority to furnish information to the Security Council and to assist the Security Council upon the latter's request, for example, if economic sanctions should be under consideration.

The secretary-general of the United Nations has, of course, a general interest in all aspects of the United Nations, as he and the Secretariat serve all organs and provide the physical machinery as well as the co-ordinating mechanism for its operations.

The secretary-general has a special interest in civil-military relations, through his authority under Article 99 to bring to the attention of the Security Council any matter which in his opinion may endanger international peace and security.

The process of keeping in close touch with the troubles of the world which may endanger peace and of reaching conclusions as to whether he should act under this authority inevitably involves the secretary-general to some degree in the military aspects of the solution of matters which he brings to the council's attention. However, the organs of the United Nations which are primarily concerned with civil-military relations are the Security Council and its subsidiary, the Military Staff Committee.

The Security Council, as you know, consists of eleven members, five of which are permanent members and six of which are elected by the General Assembly for terms of two years. You also know of the special position of the permanent members in the Security Council. All nonprocedural decisions of the Security Council, which would certainly include any decision relating to the use of military force, require an affirmative vote of seven members, including the concurring votes of the five permanent members.

The Security Council is the organ of the United Nations that has primary responsibility for the maintenance of international peace and security. The most important difference between the Security Council and previous international organizations with like responsibilities is that the Security Council has been endowed with weapons designed to enforce the maintenance of peace. The most powerful of those weapons is the right to use armed forces to maintain or restore international peace and security. In order for this weapon to be an effective one, it was necessary to provide in the Charter a method both of creating and of actually using such armed forces and a technical staff to direct them. The Charter attempts to accomplish this end through the instrumentality of a Military Staff Committee.

The Military Staff Committee consists of the chiefs of staff of the permanent members of the Security Council, the five great powers, or their representatives. Any member of the United Nations not permanently represented on the committee shall be invited by the committee to be associated with it when the efficient dispatch of its responsibilities requires the participation of that member in its work.

Under the Charter the Military Staff Committee assists the Security Council on all questions relating to the council's military requirements, the management and command of forces placed at its disposal, and the regulation of armaments and possible disarmament. The committee has the responsibility under the council for the strategic direction of any armed forces placed at the disposal of the council. It is provided that plans for the application of armed force shall be made by the Security Council with the assistance of the Military Staff Committee and that the special military agreements between members of the United Nations and the Security Council to provide armed forces, assistance, and facilities shall be negotiated by the Security Council with the assistance of the Military Staff Committee. The Military Staff Committee is further authorized, upon approval by the Security Council and after consultation with any appropriate regional agencies, to establish regional subcommittees. This is the substance of the Charter provisions concerning the Military Staff Committee.

As I have said, this is one of the pioneer fields of the United Nations. Never before has a world organization been faced with the problem of creating machinery for the international application of armed force to maintain or restore peace. As the Secretary of State pointed out in his report to the President on the results of the San Francisco Conference, this apparent innovation is in reality but one of the many examples in which the experience of the war was drawn upon in drafting the Charter. What was done was simply to take the idea of the Combined British-American Chiefs of Staff, which played such an important strategic part in winning the war, and expand it to include the five permanent members.

Obviously, a Military Committee representing all members, or even the eleven members on the Security Council, would have made a cumbersome and ineffective piece of military machinery. It was decided, therefore, to limit the membership of the Military Staff Committee to the five great powers which were given permanent seats in the Council and who also would, in the event of any action to maintain the peace, presumably again contribute the major share of any military forces which were used. These are the same countries which have a veto power in the Security Council so that in any event their agreement on military questions would have to be obtained before any action could be taken.

As the only military organ in the United Nations, the Military Staff Committee has a somewhat different structure and organization from the other bodies. For example, all the other organs of the United Nations are served by an impartial international secretariat responsible to the secretary-general, Trygve Lie. In the case of the Military Staff Committee, the Secretariat is made up of primarily military officers attached to the five delegations, and they are responsible *not* to the secretary-general but to the heads of their delegations. In this respect the Military Staff Committee follows the precedent of the wartime Combined Chiefs of Staff. The use of this device, while perhaps somewhat unwieldy, assures that all members of the Military Staff Committee have an equal voice in all aspects of the Secretariat's work. It also insures the complete secrecy necessary to the establishment of relations of trust and confidence between the members of the committee. The chairmanship of the Military Staff Committee rotates each month between the five members, and the position of principle secretary follows in the same rotation.

I could speculate, but not profitably, about the difficulty of reconciling an autonomous military organization which functions pursuant to Charter provisions with what we are prone to call sound administrative principles. Ambiguous lines of authority; the different composition of the council and the committee; and the planning, logistic, operational, and command functions of the committee present their obvious administrative anomalies; but perhaps it is altogether premature to speculate in detail on these possible difficulties.

The committee has organized itself and submitted to the Security Council for its approval a statute and rules of procedure. The treatment of the vital problem of unanimity in these rules of procedure is very interesting. Unless unanimity is obtained, a report of the Military Staff Committee to the Security Council cannot be considered as the committee recommendation. However, the report will nevertheless be submitted to the Security Council with all parties making such statements as they desire. The statute and rules of procedure have not yet been finally approved by the Security Council but are being used provisionally.

Perhaps it is worth noting some of the extremely intricate problems which the United States confronts as a result of its representation on the Military Staff Committee. I believe that all these problems can be summed up in one convenient, over-worked word—"co-ordination." How to achieve a proper co-ordination of the United States representation? The United States has three representatives on the Military Staff Committee: one from the Army, one from the Navy, and one from the Air Forces. They have only one vote, however, and must therefore always agree in advance. In case of serious disagreement between the services or between them and the State Department, the only authority who can make a decision is the president.

But there are additional problems of co-ordination. The United States representative on the Security Council is a civilian, and under the United States Participation Act receives his instructions from the president acting through the secretary of state. The Military Staff Committee reports to the Security Council, yet the United States representatives on the Military Staff Committee are subject to the direction of the president, acting through the Joint Chiefs of Staff. No formal machinery for co-ordination is necessary at the headquarters of the United Nations because the military representatives of the United States on the Military Staff Committee also act as the military advisers to the United States representative on the Security Council and are in daily contact on all their mutual problems. In Washington the problem has been met by the use of the so-called State, War, and Navy Committee for co-ordination of the policies of the three departments in this field. This committee was created during the war by the agreement of the departments and with the approval of the President; but it lacks any statutory authorization. It may be necessary to arrange further procedures for co-ordination in Washington, and it is my understanding that legislation is being suggested in Congress to provide for the permanent continuance of the State, War, and Navy Committee, which has done a remarkable piece of work in its short but extremely active life.

Most experts have long since agreed that, until an international organization has international force to back it, it cannot have much international authority in the last analysis. But to implement such a conclusion is by no means simple, and I hope that what I have said gives you at least a crude picture of some of the problems involved in introducing an international military committee, for the first time, as a formal part of an international organization for the maintenance of peace. These problems are, however, clearly secondary in importance, and I should like to pass now to a brief discussion of some of the important substantive problems which face the Military Staff Committee and the Security Council jointly and of the part which the Military Committee Staff may be expected to play in the future of the United Nations organization.

In the first place, as I have already said, the Military Staff Committee has been operating only since February and there is therefore almost no experience on which to draw. Progress has been slow; most of the decisions in the field of civilian-military relations between the Security Council and the Military Staff Committee remain for the future. What little has been accomplished so far has not yet been fully disclosed. All I can do, therefore, is to explain to you some of the problems which I believe face the Military Staff Committee and the Security Council in the future and possibly comment on the advantages and disadvantages of some of the possible different solutions of those problems.

The main problem before the Military Staff Committee at the present time is that of preparing the groundwork for the special military agreements for the provision of armed forces by the members of the United Nations. Last February the Security Council issued a directive to the Military Staff Committee to examine, as its first task from the military point of view, the provisions of Article 43 of the Charter and to submit the results of the study and its recommendations to the council. You will recall that Article 43 provides that member-nations will make available to the Security Council forces, assistance, facilities, including rights of passage, on its call, in accordance with agreements governing the number, types of forces, location, degree of readiness, and the nature of facilities and assistance.

The Military Staff Committee decided that as a first step toward the accomplishment of this task it should formulate recommendations to the Security Council as to the basic principles which should govern its proposals. Last spring all the members of the committee except the delegation from the Soviet Union submitted statements of principle as a basis for discussion. In addition, the United States submitted a model form of agreement between the Security Council and the various member-nations for the provision of military forces and assistance. I believe it has been reported that the United States at that time tentatively offered to earmark for U.N. use two divisions of troops, two naval task groups, and fifteen or twenty air groups of bombers and long-range fighters. After considerable delay, the U.S.S.R. last month likewise submitted a paper which approached the subject from a different angle than the other statements.

In any case, little progress has been made toward agreement in the Military Staff Committee on these fundamental principles, and it is a subject difficult to discuss because neither the documents nor their substance has been made public. But it is not too difficult to see some of the problems before the Military Staff Committee and the Security Council in relation to this question of military agreements.

The first problem, of course, will be to determine and to define the purposes for which these forces are to be used. These purposes will help to determine the size, nature, and composition of the forces involved.

As I have pointed out, while it is a permanent organ created by the Charter, the Military Staff Committee is basically an adviser to, and an executive arm of, the Security Council. As such, its functions necessarily are limited by the nature and capabilities of the Security Council itself. I think it fair to say that the most fundamental principle of the Security Council's organization with reference to its duties as an enforcement agency and director of the Military Staff Committee is the requirement of unanimity among the permanent members of the Security Council. It is essential to understand the implications of this rule in order to be able to think clearly about the purposes and functions of the Military Staff Committee itself.

As a result of the rule of unanimity—the veto, as it is commonly called—we can exclude from the very beginning any idea that the Security Council will ever be in a position to take enforcement action against one of its permanent members. It is inconceivable that a permanent member would ever agree to such action. The Military Staff Committee must therefore accept as a fundamental of its very being and of its planning in regard to the use of armed forces that it will never be called upon to act against one of the Big Five. Furthermore, it is unlikely that it will act against a country which enjoys the protection of one of the Big Five. But, of course, one cannot know whether a particular state which would enjoy the protection, or immunization, of a great power's veto today will do so tomorrow.

In any case, in our present-day world the unanimity rule seems to narrow the field for military action by the United Nations to a considerable degree. I think that we must be careful, however, not to press too far the conclusion that U.N. military enforcement is of little value. The founders of the United Nations at San Francisco had very clearly in mind, for example, that one of the primary purposes of the United Nations organization would be in the relatively distant future to assure that Germany and Japan would never be allowed to commence a new war of aggression against mankind. I think there is little doubt that, when peace with Germany and Japan has been made and long-term arrangements are under consideration to guarantee that peace, the machinery of the Security Council and its Military Staff Committee will be the appropriate instrument for the protection of the world against a new aggression by those states.

After determining and defining the purposes for which these forces are to be used, the Military Staff Committee will, I assume, have to agree upon some principles about the nature of the proposed world police force. Should it be a fully internationalized professional standing army, navy, and air force wearing international uniforms, with an independent command subject to the control of the Security Council? Or, on the other hand, should it be merely a pledge of military assistance by member-nations? The Charter goes a considerable way in settling the answer to this problem. The United Nations at San Francisco in effect decided that they did not want a permanent international police force, that the obstacles—financial, psychological, and political—were too great. I think it was a sound decision. The world was not at that time, nor is it today, ready to create an international standing army. Such a development must follow and not precede the creation of world government on the political level.

In any case, the United Nations Charter provides that all the members undertake to make available to the Security Council on its call and in accordance with special agreements certain armed forces, assistance, and facilities. The concept is, as I understand it, that each nation will pledge a definite contingent of armed forces which it will hold available for use by the Security Council at all times. When called for by the council, they would act under the strategic directives of the Security Council and the Military Staff Committee. Presumably they would retain their own identity, would continue to be led by their own commanders, and would remain on their own territory until called for by the Security Council. There is little consideration in immediate prospect, I would guess, for permanent mixed international garrisons at strategic bases around the world. But the international zone of Trieste will afford an example of perpetual United Nations military responsibility under the Security Council.

There remain a number of other difficult problems which the Military Staff Committee must study. What should be the size and strength of the total force made available to the United Nations? On the one hand, it is, of course, desirable that the force should be sufficiently strong so that its very existence and the constant threat of its use by the Security Council would deter any aggression. On the other hand, it must be remembered that a decision of the Security Council to use force would require the unanimous agreement of the five great powers, together with at least two others. Realistically, it is hardly conceivable that any nation would dare oppose a decision of the Security Council which was backed by all the available resources of the Big Five. It might be argued, therefore, that the total armed forces pledged to the Security Council need not be large. Furthermore, it is, of course, in the general interest that the nations maintain no larger forces than are necessary. But the Military Staff Committee will have to take into consideration that not all the pledged forces could be made available quickly at any particular part of the earth where they might be required. I should not imagine that the total pledged forces would need to exceed one million men, in the light of all the considerations.

Other questions concern the number and type of contingents that would be made available, the relative size of the contingents of each country, their state of readiness, facilities, logistic requirements, location, etc. For example, to take only one aspect: Should each of the Big Five agree to provide contingents of roughly equal size? If so, how are we to determine the relative size or power of a division of ground troops pledged by Russia and a fleet of B-29's or a naval task force or even an atom bomb pledged by the United States? Again, what proportion of the total forces should be provided by the Big Five?

I hardly need add that the work of the Atomic Energy Commission and any subsidiary organization of the United Nations which may ultimately be formed as a result of its recommendations is a field in which the military have vital interests. It would seem likely that some arrangements will ultimately be worked out for military participation. It is entirely clear that as far as the United States is concerned, the War and Navy departments have been made a formal part of our organization dealing with this matter. Mr. Baruch has on his staff several military men, and I understand that the American representatives of the Military Staff Committee have also been acting as his advisers.

Another interesting problem is that dealing with the question of whether these United Nations forces should be made available to the Security Council before a decision by the council that a threat to the peace actually exists. It would, I suppose, make for efficiency in the case of a crisis if the contingents of armed forces pledged by the various countries were made available to the Security Council for exercises so that mechanisms of command could be organized and in existence well in advance of any necessity for their use. As in other cases, action by the United Nations to mobilize its armed forces would have a very healthful effect. If forces cannot be mobilized, so to speak, until the council has taken action under Article 39, much precious time may be lost. From my own experience in the Navy Department before and during the war, I can recall only too well how difficult it was to get our expansion and organization program under way until after Pearl Harbor.

On the other hand, there are clearly strong arguments for requiring the Security Council to reach a decision that a threat to the peace exists and that other less drastic measures, such as imposition of diplomatic and economic sanctions, have failed or are likely to fail before actually calling upon member-nations to place their contingents under the strategic direction of the Council and the Military Staff Committee. In this connection, I should remind you that the Charter contains a provision requiring members to hold national air-force contingents immediately available to enable the U.N. to take urgent military measures. Properly implemented, this provision might be very useful and provide some time cushion.

Then there will also be problems relating to the possible zonal use of the contingents provided by various nations. Should the forces of certain nations be called upon first, or possibly even exclusively, in connection with trouble in areas near these particular countries? It may be that some countries will prefer not to have their troops called upon, in the first instance at least, in connection with troubles in distant places. This question brings up directly the position of the United States in relation to the use of force in the Western Hemisphere and our commitments under the Act of Chapultepec in regard to the collective maintenance of peace in this hemisphere.

Another interesting question is the relationship between forces which are pledged to the Security Council and the total forces which a country should maintain in its military establishment. I believe the concept prevalent at San Francisco was that a country would commit to the United Nations only a part of its total force. One of the considerations involved in coming to a conclusion on this matter will be whether a country may use for its own purposes the contingents which it has pledged to the Security Council without the Security Council's consent. If it cannot use such forces without the Security Council's consent, it will probably desire to maintain a larger total establishment than would otherwise be the case. On the other hand, it has been suggested that the entire forces of every member of the United Nations should be committed to the United Nations Security Council. The arguments in support of this position are that the United Nations will defend all the countries from attack and that therefore no separate forces are required for legitimate purposes. If the United Nations failed to take action to protect any particular country, that country would, of course, be entirely free to use all its available forces to protect itself. Furthermore, neighboring countries would also be free to come to its support in accordance with the provisions of Article 51 of the Charter, protecting the inherent right of individual or collective self-defense.

The question is directly related to the problem of the regulation or armaments and disarmament. In connection with the regulation of armaments, appropriate relationships between forces pledged to the Security Council and a nation's total forces may be established. If such ratios are to be established in the future, it is possible that some nations might prefer to increase rather than to decrease the size of the contingents made available to the Security Council or even the size of certain categories of forces within their total contingents.

These are but some of the problems which are conspicuously apparent in connection with the organization of the United Nations armed forces. I think it is clear that they are not all in cases exclusively military problems but in reality are largely political. They will call for the closest possible relations between the civilian authorities of the various countries concerned and their military advisers, as well as the closest relations between the Security Council and its Military Staff Committee. I can see nothing but beneficial results from this continuous contact between the higher ranks of military and civilian officials at both the national and international levels.

It is apparent that there are many serious obstacles facing those within the United Nations organization who are pioneering in this field of civilian-military relationship. The problems of a political-military nature which must be jointly solved by the soldiers and the statesmen are complex and delicate and far reaching. They must be solved before the United Nations will have an effective police force. If they are solved, the wholesome effect of the creation as part of the United Nations of a military arm will, I dare say, be evident in the future in ways which are not apparent now when we are preoccupied with the limitations on its usefulness inherent in the unanimity requirement among the Big Five powers. That the Military Staff Committee has made little progress on its enormous task is not surprising. Its difficulties are, in part at least, a reflection of the problems of the Security Council and the U.N. itself—the veto, large nations versus small nations, regionalism, bases, trusteeship, disarmament, the control of atomic energy, and the fundamental conflicts of nationalism and internationalism, of East and West. Its task probably cannot be completed and the military forces of U.N. organized in accordance with the Charter until a general political settlement has been reached, until the treaties have been concluded and peace and stability have come at last.

Happily, the prospects in that direction look brighter. In the meanwhile, and it is something generally overlooked, the five great powers have an obligation under Article 106 to maintain international peace until the armed-forces agreements can be completed. And in the meanwhile, something else is happening. The top soldiers and sailors of the world are meeting together and working together. Civilians have been work-

ing together internationally for years. They are working together in the other organs in the U.N. in a multitude of fields.
And now, for almost the first time, this healthy habit of working together has been extended to the military. There is something hopeful in that. Its effect on a future which depends so
much on faith and good will in great-power relationships may
be of incalculable value.

And now, before I conclude, I have been asked to discuss
the prospects for disarmament action at this session of the
General Assembly.

I will be brief. You will recall that Mr. Molotov on October
29 said to the General Assembly that, now that the aggressors
had been disarmed, the time had come to carry out a general
restriction of armaments. Senator Austin promptly replied
that the United States was prepared to co-operate fully in
disarmament, subject to "effective safeguards by way of inspection and other means to protect complying states against
the hazards of violation and evasion."

That, I think it is safe to say, will be our position in the
assembly. The assembly, it should be remembered, can only
make recommendations regarding principles governing disarmament and the regulation of armaments. It is for the
the Security Council, with the assistance of the Military Staff
Committee, to formulate plans for the regulation of armaments. We believe that this assembly should adopt a resolution to start the machinery of disarmament and regulation in
motion, based on those principles of effective safeguards
against violation of any disarmament treaty, and airtight as-
surances that all nations will fulfil equally and on schedule
any arms-reduction commitments.

As in the case of atomic-energy control, which is, in part, an
armament problem with respect to a single weapon, the general disarmament problem will again be effective international
controls. Because one thing is quite certain: This country will

never disarm unilaterally again. I doubt whether any Congress will be more intent on economy than on security and peace. I doubt whether any Congress will undermine our bargaining power, enfeeble us by further reducing our military and naval strength, and disarm us unilaterally.

Whether a general armament regulation should be handled by a new special commission of U.N., as in the case of atomic-energy regulation, or by the same commission, or by the Security Council itself is among questions under current consideration.

The control problems presented by any general disarmament or regulation program multiply the difficulties already encountered in reaching agreement on atomic-energy control. Some weapons must be forbidden as weapons but developed for their peaceful utility—atomic energy, perhaps rockets and guided missiles. Others, artillery, for example, have less apparent peaceful utility. An effective system of international controls must be developed to fit all the land, sea, and air weapons. Some will be easy, some very difficult.

Obviously, the Military Staff Committee's task of working out principles and agreements for the provision of armed forces, the Atomic Energy Commission's task, and the program for disarmament are all parts of the whole problem of armament regulation. Our position on international atomic control and on the basic requirement for safeguards by inspection or otherwise has been made very clear. It is interesting to recall in contemplation of this over-all attack on the problem or armaments that Mr. Litvinov, at the disarmament conferences in 1929 and 1932, called for a system of international inspection to insure compliance with his bold and forward-looking proposals for multilateral disarmament.

I will not attempt to estimate the prospects for real progress all along the whole disarmament front. But I suppose it is a safe assumption that progress will depend in large measure on a general political settlement, stability, and confidence.

In any event, the Soviet proposal is not only welcome but an encouraging augury for the future. And our delegation to the General Assembly will make positive proposals for this first great step forward toward the ultimate goal—that, in order to promote peace and security with the least diversion for armaments of human and economic resources, each nation shall need and have only enough armed forces to fulfil its pledge to the United Nations and to insure domestic tranquillity.

The goal may be distant, but the exploratory work of the Military Staff Committee, the Atomic Energy Commission, and soon a new body on general arms' regulation are tangible products of the Charter and the machinery of the United Nations that no cynic can ignore.

SECURITY WITHOUT MILITARISM: PRESERV-
ING CIVILIAN CONTROL IN AMERICAN
POLITICAL INSTITUTIONS

CHARLES E. MERRIAM

✻

THIS is a theme which in some ways is very old and in
some ways very new. From the beginning of American
political life the supremacy of civil over military authority
has been recognized as a cardinal principle of our political
faith, enunciated over and over again by national leaders
from General Washington down to General Eisenhower. General Washington was also President Washington, but the
General was not interested in a military dictatorship. Nor did
General Andrew Jackson concern himself with bolstering the
powers of President Jackson by the use of armed forces. General Ulysses Grant, head of the most powerful army in his
time, also became president but was not interested in supple-
menting his political authority by military means. Incidentally, General Grant left the army, he said, because he did not
like discipline; nor did he like the Mexican War in which he
was engaged, regarding it as an unjust war. Certainly it never
entered into the head of General Pershing that he might seize
political control through the tremendous military forces he
had once commanded. Nor did it occur to anyone that the
genial General Eisenhower is interested in reaching political
control by employing military strength, even when he emerges
as the head of the most formidable armed forces ever assembled
in the history of the human race. When the issue of civilian or
military control over the development of atomic energy was

156

raging in Washington, it was one of our own University of Chicago professors, Thorfin R. Hogness, who approached General Eisenhower and found that he was strongly in favor of civilian control—a surprising conclusion to some who had assumed that the Army would naturally favor military control. Some army men did, to be sure, but not this general.

Militarism as a dominating influence in national policy has never been a significant factor in American public life. In many European countries the army has been the instrument of despotic government, openly employed for the purposes of a special group or class. England, to be sure, carried on a perpetual struggle between military-naval forces and democratic groups after the English revolutions. This was also true in western European countries in the nineteenth century. Germany was the outstanding example of military rule not as an instrument of civil policy but as a tool of a special group.

Quincy Wright pointed out previously in this series that the military principle and the democratic principle stand in direct opposition to each other. The military hierarchy involves authority from the top down, while the democratic systems are based on the consent of the governed from the grass roots up. The military principle develops the idea of discipline and unquestioning obedience. Democratic political society is based upon the consent of the governed, freely given. In the nature of the case, most military orders are not subject to judicial review, nor is a military trial reviewable at the time, whatever may happen afterward. Mussolini's favorite phrase was "Believe, obey, fight." Democracies also, as they have shown on more than one occasion, can believe, obey, and fight—but in a framework of common consent, in a spirit of liberty and equality and social justice.

Wright analyzed keenly the inherent difficulties in the development of militarism, which may now be regarded as even greater than ever, in view of the technological situation emerging. He said:

Nonprofessionals have difficulty in shaking from the back of their minds the thought that "all's well that ends well" and that maybe there is virtue in improvising defense after emergencies have arisen. While they would admit that such improvisation has its cost, it may have the advantage of escaping the professional's reluctance to abandon obsolete methods; his hesitation to utilize the most advanced science, invention, and engineering; and his prejudice against recommendations of able nonprofessional minds. Improvisation may have the virtue of escaping the dead hand of tradition and routine; the virtue of invoking a national sense of participation and initiative in business, labor, agriculture, and society as a whole; the virtue of stimulating individual self-reliance; and the virtue of assuring that politics—the art of changing the minds of men, whether those men are nationals, allies, neutrals, or enemies—will remain the master-art, of which the use of force is only one instrument.

But, of course, it is important to distinguish between military functions and militarism. Militarism, like other forms of bureaucracy, is an occupational disease, which is a departure from, rather than a development of, its true function. The military function is the organized use of force in internal or international relations, and its main lines of policy should be politically determined in a sound system. When force determines the ends and purposes of the state, we are headed for tyranny and injustice and for a reversal of the objectives of government. The temptation of every function is, naturally, to expand its area of influence without adequate regard for the common good taken as a whole.

There are virtues within the legitimate scope of military functions; courage, sacrifice, tenacity, alertness, are among these attributes encouraged in military groups under the most favorable circumstances, as over against cowardice, selfishness, indifference, weak will. If and when force is eliminated as a means of human adjustment, military organization and authority retreat into the background. Meanwhile force is employed in self-defense to make possible the conditions under which reason and co-operation may live and advance to higher levels.

The organization of violence is a heady drink, to be sure, but civilization tends to leave it behind in the race for human evolution. In the family, in the school, in labor, we tend to substitute other methods of prevention—medication, mediation, trouble-shooting, and intimate understanding—which make the lash, the stocks, beatings and brandings, and segregation disappear from general use, along with duels and other forms of private war. (Mass destruction now looms as the next obstacle to peace.)

In this connection Colonel T. V. Smith outlined the work of the A.M.G. in preparing populations for the organization and use of democratic systems of governments in Italy, Germany, Japan. In these cases the army force is utilized for the purpose of producing conditions under which the consent of the governed may operate. Military strength is used for the very purpose of making military strength unnecessary or reducible to a bare minimum. The army thus becomes no longer the agency of violence as such or of obedience and discipline as such but a system in which equality and co-operation are the essential elements. Both Paul Appleby and Dixon Wecter emphasized the importance of broad civilian training directed toward effective understanding of national problems in economics and politics in their military setting. Wecter said:

A generation which faced its disillusionment before the shooting began—which had sometimes taken the Oxford pledge of pacifism . . . appeared, at least in segments, to be of more skeptical temper and with more sober responsibility than any articulate groups remembered from earlier wars. . . . Will the veteran and his civilian neighbor [asked Wecter] ever begin to question the rightfulness, the necessity of the war lately ended, as happened in the wake of the previous World War?

If there is need of broad and more fundamental civic education for the civilian population, it may also be contended that the training of the military should likewise be set on a broader and firmer basis of economics, politics, and social sciences.

In his related discussion Hanson Baldwin dealt with the recruitment and training of the armed forces. His lessons of the last war are vividly stated:

1. Our educational-cultural society between wars fostered a lost generation not mentally or spiritually prepared for war.

2. Victory was not won by big battalions but by big factories.

3. It took longer to equip armies than it did to train them.

4. Technological revolution in warfare is changing our old concepts of strategy in the direction of offense rather than of defense.

5. The new military forces must be full-time professionals and not part-time soldiers.

Baldwin discussed in detail what kind of military establishment is needed, as to size, type, method of raising forces, and modes of training. Concerning compulsory peacetime military training, he reached the conclusion that this was neither a progressive measure nor for the over-all good of the nation nor would it promote international understanding and peace. As in the case of Appleby, Baldwin emphasized the importance, both for soldiers and civilians, of understanding "what it is all about."

A number of readjustments in American institutions are imperatively necessary to preserve the balance between civil and military authority, to further the establishment of national security. Among these are the following:

1. The old-time ideas of the organization of the Department of State have been outdated by modern developments. What now is the relation of the State Department to the Department of Commerce or to the Department of Agriculture or to the

Department of Labor or to the Treasury? All of these are equally important in our national contacts and responsibilities. Beyond that, what should be the relation of the State Department to the Army, the Navy, and the Air Force of the United States? There has been much discussion of the establishment of a department of national defense or of a defense council. But of even greater importance is the reorganization of the Department of State in the modern world order. Important efforts have been made to bridge over this gap by useful coordinating committees, but these still leave much to be desired. The very intelligent discussion of this topic by Appleby was an important contribution to the solution of the problem. He emphasized (*a*) the significance of interstaff relations in military control and operation and the importance of developing a sufficient pool of national political figures actually prepared for high executive or general-staff posts and (*b*) the question of the adequacy of the basic political philosophy held by the individuals concerned. "Civilian control," he said, "is never finally achieved but poses a continuing problem requiring constant watchfulness."

The effective reorganization of external affairs is a problem of prime importance not to be lightly handled or dismissed. Very valuable inquiries have recently been made in this field, and others will no doubt be made in the not too distant future.

2. Other important developments are found in (*a*) the maintenance of civilian control over industrial production in war times as well as in peace (when President Roosevelt announced plans for a hundred thousand airplanes a year, the statement was not taken too seriously by the enemy or even by us; but the attainment of this volume of production and of like volumes in other fields was of tremendous importance in determining the outcome of the struggle) and (*b*) civilian control of research, regarded as fundamental both in peace and in

war time. With the development of atomic energy this is, of course, more important than ever, and specific reference will be made to this topic a little later. Obviously Appleby and others do not mean that no research should be conducted by the Army and Navy but that the guiding controls should not be in military hands. This has been emphasized in recent times by the creation of the Atomic Energy Commission and the strongly backed bill for a national research foundation. This last proposal fell by the wayside in the Seventy-ninth Congress, but it is likely to be revived and made effective in the near future. In this connection, Waldemar Kaempffert stressed the need for organization in science, particularly the establishment of a National Science Foundation. He further emphasized the need for social science in the field of research:

The Atomic Energy Commission of the United Nations does not lean so heavily as it should on the social scientists. The inquiries of that body have been conducted largely by physicists, the heads of industrial corporations, and well-meaning public-spirited citizens who know nothing of the forces that shape history. And the larger issue of abolishing war itself has hardly been touched—an issue that can hardly be left to the military or to the diplomats who serve national interests or to manufacturing corporations. It is an issue that must be studied by social scientists with the aid of . . . professional soldiers, natural scientists, and technologists. It is surely a paradox that we enlisted the aid of psychologists and social scientists in making the most of operational research during the war but still decline to use it in deciding the most momentous issues that mankind must face.

From a slightly different point of view, attention has been given in this series of lectures to the danger from military-minded congressional committees on the Army and Navy. Appleby particularly directed attention to the fact that control of committees in Congress might fall into the hands of civilians who are more sympathetic with military demands than the occasion might require. In such a case civilian control, he thought, would be seriously weakened through over-emphasis on, or overattention to, the requirements for military defense. It could, of course, be pointed out that at various times the opposite has been the case, as shown by President Truman's Special Committee To Investigate the National Defense Program, while he was a member of the Senate Committee on Military Affairs. All this, however, is in agreement with Appleby's thesis that eternal vigilance is the price of effective civilian control.

In the emerging atomic age the problem of maintaining security without losing our liberties becomes of greater importance than ever before. We are now confronted by a revolution dimming in meaning all previous revolutions rolled into one.

First of all, the meaning of atomic energies is often wholly misunderstood. The real marvel is not that these vast forces exist but that they are found and harnessed by the human mind. The real explosive force is that of the mind that unleashed these giants and made them available for the service of mankind. The mind is king, not the atom. We trapped the atom; we have mastered some secrets of its latent forces not by accident but by deliberate design, by organization and ingenuity. We may marvel at the display of physical force, but the deeper force of mind made this triumph possible and will bring still greater triumphs as we move along through eras of discovery and invention. The atomic bomb is a symbol of death and destruction; but it may also be a symbol of life, of construction, of a germinal principle.

We have now to consider a whole body of new relationships. Armies wish to control these new engines of wholesale disaster for purposes of national and world security. Industries are deeply concerned with the production and proliferation of atomic energies alike for wartime and for peacetime application. The atomic scientists who brought the atomic bomb into the world are smitten with a sense of responsibility for the new forces of destruction. They also fear that the requirements of military secrecy may result in the failure to discover and disseminate new truth. They find the extension of wartime restrictions into peacetime places an intolerable burden upon the free development of science.

Civilians are concerned not only with the catastrophic consequences of atomic warfare but with the possible loss of their liberty in the new situation. Never before have such terrific engines of destruction been placed in human hands with the clear possibility of letting them loose upon the world.

Decisions of vast moment must be made—decisions the effect of which cannot be undone and decisions which must be made in the twinkling of an eye—without time for parliamentary debates or judicial reviews.

How will it be possible to curb or check the holders of such titanic powers? What if the holders of brief authority attempt to convert their position into permanent tyrannical control? What becomes of the consent of the governed under these circumstances? Of democratic institutions, however successful in the past?

Even if we obtain security from abroad, how can we insure security and liberty at home? What is there to prevent the military authorities or the scientists or the industralists or some combination of interests from taking over the whole population and subduing the many to the dominance of the few?

Victory over the enemy under such circumstances may be as dangerous as defeat. It is conceivable that a new type of militarism might emerge with greater power than any in human history. With a twist of the wrist, perhaps whole communities might be wiped out in an instant. Accountability will be difficult to bring about, except by new attitudes and new inventions and by the selection of men of known and tested reliability and trustworthiness, equal to unparalleled temptations.

If no one can be trusted, then the community has no sound basis or reason for existence. It was often possible historically for one untrustworthy person to poison the spring waters, to set fire to the sleeping village, to murder men as they awoke from their dreams. So some evil genius might enslave or destroy his associates with the new and dread weapons of neutronics. The basic guaranty of security in such case is not institutional or mechanical checks but the deeper roots of human nature from which association arises. Slavery and suicide are always in the background of human nature, individual or associational. Here again it is plain that the basis of authority is not force alone but justice—consent based upon experience and expectation.

Meanwhile we build such institutions as we may to guard against these contingencies:

1. We have built the A.E.C. for the control of atomic energies in the United States and have provided for civilian control of this agency, with liaison with military officials, scientists, political representatives in Congress, and with such other agencies as may be set up from time to time. We must note again the important role of General Eisenhower.

2. We have proposed to the U.N. the A.E.A. for the world control of atomic energies. This agency might well become one of the most significant institutions in-the history of mankind as the arbiter of human disputes and disagreements—an important step toward the elimination of violence.

Of itself this is only a negative measure, with the limited results involved in negations of this and other types. But this is only one side of the picture. On the other side is the possibility of peacetime uses of atomic energy in raising the standards of human living and human hope. Two billions were spent on the atomic bomb. If an equal amount were devoted to the pursuit of the peacetime uses of these same and other related energies, the desert might blossom as the rose. This presupposes that the drive toward success in this area is as bold as the drive toward the bomb, that the knights of Doubting Castle will not conjure up untold difficulties from the depths of timidity and pessimism.

Real security cannot be obtained on an isolated basis, either with or without militarism. The jural order of the world is the essential basis of safety of individuals and for nations. In my *Systematic Politics* I have dwelt upon this at great length and will not repeat the guiding considerations here. The United Nations points the way by which we may advance to a yet more fully developed world order on a higher and more effective level.

In his discussion of "Civil-Military Relations in the United Nations," Adlai Stevenson dwelt upon the work of the Security Council and of the Military Staff Committee of the U.N., consisting of the chiefs of staff of the permanent members of the Security Council. Their work and problems are clearly analyzed by Stevenson in his concise statement. Should this force, for example, be an internationalized professional army or a pledge of assistance by member-nations? As you know, the answer was the latter; however, Wright dissented strongly from this conclusion. What should be the size and strength of the forces available? What is the relation of this agency to the A.E.C.? To the U.N.? And so forth. Many of these problems, Stevenson points out, are largely political in nature or partly so. Civilians have been working together internationally for many years. Now "the top soldiers and sailors of the world are meeting together and working together," says Stevenson.

Beyond this lies the general problem of disarmament. This country declared our willingness to co-operate fully in disarmament "subject to effective safeguards by way of inspection and other means to protect complying states against the hazards of violation and evasion." Whether general armament regulation should be handled by a new special commission of the U.N., as in the case of atomic energy, or by the same commission or by the Security Council itself is a question under current consideration. Air controls, energy controls, and rocket and other missile controls are certain to present the most difficult of questions; but positive progress, Stevenson finds, is in the making, even though the results may thus far be meager.

Of very great significance are other problems not dwelt upon in this series. Among them are (1) the organization and powers of the International Court of Justice, survival from earlier institutional efforts, and (2) the recent proposal of Mr. Francis Biddle for a law forbidding aggressive war with appropriate sanctions applicable in case of violation of the law. Obviously such a law would not be stronger than the solidarity of the associated powers. That these projects are closely related to security in the United States and elsewhere requires no argument here.

But there are other pertinent considerations affecting our security in the jural order of the world. Some of these may be noted here:

1. A world community rests upon a common consciousness of right and wrong. What has the community in common? What is the common bond of unity? Bills of rights are in a sense the other side of bills of wrongs in American history as elsewhere. Tell us what are the wrongs of men and we can construct a bill of human world rights. The U.N. Commission on Human Rights is at work on this important problem, and it is to be hoped that substantial progress will be made in the very near future. If and when there is agreement on the basic rights of man, there will then arise the question as to the ways

and means of implementing these rights effectively in the lives of men everywhere.

2. A second feature of far-reaching importance is the functional administrative authorities in a world agency. In fields such as finance, trade, health, food, living and working conditions, cultural activities, there are broad possibilities of co-operative human action. U.N.E.S.C.O. is one of the prime examples of agencies of this type. Around it will doubtless spring up many related and collateral agencies with purposes allied to that of U.N.E.S.C.O.

3. The future of human association in the world community depends not alone on guns and laws, important as they may be at times, but on contributions made to the welfare of mankind through association. Here we come inevitably upon plans for maximum production everywhere, upon minimum standards of human existence, upon a fair share of the growing gains of civilization for all men, upon a floor for the basic conditions upon which human liberty, equality, justice, rest—an atmosphere in which they live and move and have their being. Fortunately, the Economic and Social Council of the U.N. is at work on these far-reaching problems.

Security is not negative in nature but positive; not static but dynamic; not merely freedom from something, as from fear of hunger, but freedom of initiative, opportunity, the fullest expression of the human personality—an open road for life, liberty, and the pursuit of happiness.

An analysis of recent trends and of emerging forces leads to the conclusion that American security and peace are conditioned upon: (1) one world or none, (2) 100 per cent democracy or none, and (3) unity in the fundamentals of civilization—or no civilization.

Difficult as it is for the mind to compress these alternatives and to fit them into a pattern of life, nevertheless we are swift-ly moving toward fateful decisions.

1. Security calls for one world or none. If we cannot organize a jural order of the world establishing peace among peoples, the explosive forces constantly growing more formi-dable may bring about universal destruction. No one can now prove such an outcome, but the probabilities and possibilities of destruction are constantly rising around us. On the other hand, our constructive powers are constantly increasing. There is sound reason to believe that human reason will be able to formulate implements that will put an end to anarchy and establish world order and peace. It cannot be too strongly or too often stated that world order does not mean the end of self-government, either public or private government. On the contrary, when the threat of war is removed, autonomy will flower as never before in many forms of human association, with security and opportunity for development such as had never been known.

2. Security calls for 100 per cent democracy or none. It be-comes increasingly clear that democracy cannot survive unless it is a working mechanism adapted to the changed needs of new times and of all men everywhere, of all creeds, colors, classes. If democracy cannot meet the challenge of the new day, it must give way to some other form. A democratic govern-ment cannot survive unless it can guarantee an order in which justice rules the whole social field. Attacks upon despotism have a hollow sound if they are merely means of escaping a fair distribution of the gains of civilization. Twist and turn the argument as you will, there can be no escape from the logic of democracy which brings into human life the recognition of the dignity of man, the fundamental equality of men, and the formulation of such conditions as may be necessary for the pursuit of happiness. Unless all this is understood and spelled out plainly in the lives of multitudes of men, we are merely

saying "Peace, peace, when there is no peace." This may seem to be a hard way, but we need not deceive ourselves by wishful thinking as to other and some more pleasant alternatives. We must face the fact that the alternative to democracy with a comprehensive social program is some other force which promises, however incapable of performance, what democracy does not produce. Thus the alternative is 100 per cent democracy or none.

3. Security calls for unity in the fundamentals of civilization—or no civilization. When we view the diverse cultural patterns of the modern world, the various systems of religion and institutionalized idealism, each long and tenaciously held by millions of devoted followers or worshipers, it might seem that an agreement upon any significant fundamentals is beyond the reach of reasonable hope. The diverse rituals, symbolisms, customs, devotions, of too many types are involved to make even a working hypothesis plausible. Yet, on the other hand, it is equally difficult to see how the emerging world of peace, prosperity, progress, can develop without some deeper and broader understanding of what is common to mankind. What does the world community have in common? How can there be a common code unless there is a common agreement upon values basic to the lives of all men?

It may be said that a common creed including all the folkways and the ideals of the world is impossible of attainment. However, it is not impossible that behind the creeds and the cultures of men there may be found guiding directives pointing to common values and common ideals. These patterns may fit into a type of idealism which in turn fits into a jural order of the world and into 100 per cent democracy. We know now that cultural patterns are not inherited biologically but are transmitted from generation to generation by processes of education and what is properly called "acculturation"—a long word describing a long but universal process. We now know that the stranger is not necessarily an enemy. We now know that many of the hatreds, prejudices, antipathies, whether geographical, rational, or religious, (1) have no rational basis and (2) with modern methods of technology and education may be fundamentally altered. Even the most primitive groups learn to use the results of modern mechanistic development with relative speed. Likewise, scientific methods applied to cultural patterns may also produce surprisingly rapid developments. What is lacking is not the technical ways and means but the faith and the will to do so.

The question may, of course, be raised as to who has the authority or the power to deal with the mass of mankind or what patterns would be imposed if there were authority. It is at this point that we come back to the original assertion of the importance of creating or helping to create a world community in which reason, justice, order, freedom, are in the ascendancy in human nature. This is not the occasion to set down the ways and means of achieving such a goal, but it is the time and place to assert that without some agreement upon the fundamental patterns of world civilization there is no security. The humanity we know may be shaken to pieces and destroyed by its own lack of central cohesion. The world is moving at a phenomenal pace in science, technology, education. There will not be found warriors enough or lawyers or sovereignty or sanction enough to maintain the peace and harmony of the world unless there is a broader basis of agreement on the goals of civilization. Only creative action will prevent the increase of poisonous and malevolent individuals or groups or collective scoundrels who may hurl their destructive forces and fallacies at the heart of mankind and warp world public opinion.

If it is asked, What have we to build such a castle in the air upon? the answer is the whole experience of the human race, cast in a new mold—one of reflection and a new type of action pattern. Our decendants may find it possible to live a good life—a better life—without all the clichés and ritualisms, the ideologies and the institutions of history. There was substance in these isms, and something remains; there was life, and their progeny still live and move, seeking their own expressions of vitality. We shall hold fast to that which is good. But human reason and reflection will find new lines of human advance. In a sense a new dimension has been added to human thought and human possibilities. New horizons of space and time have been broadened out over the older ones, and broader vistas of hope and faith are opened out to mankind. If wars are made in the minds of men, so too is peace.

Two grave dangers confront us in this situation: (1) that we fail to analyze and appreciate the new forces at work in the modern world, clinging to the disappearing elements in the past; justifying what is by what has been, rather than by what might be; and (2) that we take refuge in easy flights of imagination to a future so far removed as to be unattainable in our time, thus avoiding contacts with the hard present and its grim actualities. The new synthesis will not be easy to effect. It will include the best elements in many cultures, the best elements in religion, the best elements in natural and unnatural science, and the best elements in nationalism. Out of it could come a new faith in the future of mankind. But an alternative is titanic struggle that involves the whole world in savagery.

Can religion rise to these heights? If so, which and where? Can science supply the spirit and the symbolism? If so, where does it start? The world is grouping toward a hand it cannot reach, a light it cannot fully see, a beam of faith it cannot yet find and follow. Evolution points a secure and peaceful way to the new environment where we may capture and develop security and hope. But the movement itself will be revolutionary, both in thought and in the consequences of thought; and this way only lies the security of peace and the higher levels of human personality.

INDEX

✻

173

Date Due

DEC 1 1			
OCT 1 2			
NOV 2 7			
NO 31 72			
DE 4 78			
DE 3 74			
Demco 293-5			